THE UNSEEN WORLD

Angels

VOLUME

1

GOD'S INVISIBLE MESSENGERS

Don
Stewart

Angels:
God's Invisible Messengers

© 2016 By Don Stewart

Published by ETW (Educating Our World)
www.educatingourworld.com
San Dimas, California 91773
All rights reserved

English Versions Cited

The various English versions which we cite in this course, apart from the King James Version, all have copyrights. They are listed as follows.

TABLE OF CONTENTS

Angels
What The Bible Says About God's Invisible Messengers

(Volume 1)

The Bible speaks of the existence of a vast number of spirit-beings called angels. There is much superstition and ignorance surrounding these created beings. In this book we will take a look at what the Scripture says about the angels who remained faithful to the Lord; the good angels. Who are they? What do they do? How do we know they really exist?

In the second volume of our series, we will consider the topics of evil angels, demons, and the occult. We will discover that not all angels are good. In fact, while some angels chose to worship and serve God, others rebelled. This has created two major divisions of angels. From Scripture, we discover that there is a highly organized angelic army which is our spiritual enemy. This includes the demons, who are fallen angels.

The last book in our series will deal with the topic of Satan, the created spirit-being who became the devil, the adversary of the Lord.

In sum, this series will look at what the Bible has to say about the various spirit beings, both the good and the bad, that exist in a realm that is invisible to our naked eyes.

QUESTION 1

Do Angels
Actually Exist

The Bible testifies to the existence of a distinct order of heavenly beings known as angels. Who are they? What do we know about them?

From searching the Scripture, we learn the following about this most interesting of subjects.

1. THEY ARE NOT MYTHICAL CREATURES

Angels actually exist. Indeed, there is no hint in Scripture that angels are mythical creatures; they are always treated as having genuine existence.

The first mention of angels is in the Book of Genesis where the angel of the LORD appears to Hagar, the mother of Abraham's child. The Bible says.

> The angel of the LORD found Hagar near a spring in the desert; it was the spring that is beside the road to Shur (Genesis 16:7 NIV).

The last mention of angels is in the final chapter of the last book of the Bible; the Book of Revelation. It reads as follows.

> I, Jesus, have sent my angel to testify to you about these things for the churches. I am the root and the descendant of David, the bright morning star (Revelation 22:16 ESV).

ANGELS

From the first book of the Bible, until the last, the existence of angels is assumed.

2. THERE ARE MANY REFERENCES TO ANGELS IN THE SCRIPTURE

Between the first and last mention of angels in the Bible, there are literally hundreds of other references to them. Their existence is assumed everywhere in Scripture. The fact of their reality is documented in both testaments. Thirty-four books of the Bible (seventeen in each testament) speak of the existence of angels.

We also find that the activity of angels has increased as biblical history unfolded. Indeed, accounts of angelic appearances were sporadic throughout the Old Testament era until near its close. However, during the Babylonian captivity the ministry of angels became more visible.

While nothing is recorded of their activity between the testaments, the New Testament itself opens with an angelic visit from the angel Gabriel to Zacharias, the father of John the Baptist. This activity continues until the very last page of Scripture.

3. SCRIPTURE IS THE FINAL AUTHORITY CONCERNING THEIR EXISTENCE

If the Bible is what it claims to be, God's revelation of Himself to humanity, then whatever subject it speaks about, it does so with ultimate authority. Since the Scriptures clearly teach the existence of beings called angels, then it is a fact that they do exist.

4. THE AUTHORITY OF JESUS CHRIST IS AT STAKE

The existence of angels is also tied to the authority of Jesus Christ. He referred to the resurrected state of believers as being similar to that of angels.

> Jesus replied, "Your problem is that you don't know the Scriptures, and you don't know the power of God. For when the dead rise, they won't be married. They will be like the angels in heaven" (Matthew 22:29-30 NLT).

According to Jesus, those who believe in Him, will be like the angels of heaven in the sense they will not be married.

Christ also said that angels would gather believers when He returns to the earth. Matthew records Jesus saying the following.

> When the Son of Man comes in his glory, and all the angels with him, then he will sit on his glorious throne. Before him will be gathered all the nations, and he will separate people one from another as a shepherd separates the sheep from the goats (Matthew 25:31,32 ESV).

It is clear that Jesus believed in the existence of angels. Since He is the eternal God who became a human being, He would be in a position to know if they do exist. He said that they did. This settles the matter.

5. WHILE ANGELS EXIST, OUR INFORMATION ABOUT THEM IS LIMITED

The final point that we wish to make cannot be stressed too strongly. The fact that angels exist is unquestionable. Scripture clearly teaches that they exist and that they have a purpose in the plan of God. However, our knowledge about angels is limited and it is important that we understand why this is so.

THE MAIN CHARACTERS: GOD AND THE HUMAN RACE

The main characters in Scripture are God and the human race; in particular those who have believed in Him. The Bible records the existence and identity of one true God and how He has dealt with humanity. This is what the entire Bible is all about. Everything in Scripture is written for this purpose.

While telling the story of God and humanity we find that angels are mentioned from time to time. Yet, they are only mentioned when they have something to do with the overall story of Scripture. In other words, they are never mentioned for the sake of satisfying our curiosity.

Since what is revealed to us about these spirit-beings is limited, our knowledge about them will be limited. Indeed, while there are certain things which we do know there are other things which we are not told.

We must always keep this in mind when dealing with this subject, as well as any other subject that is not the main thrust of the Scripture.

In Scripture, God is teaching us about Himself and how we relate to Him. He is not attempting to give us a thorough course on angels, science or the history of nations that existed in the ancient world. It is important that this be understood.

In sum, as we examine the Bible we will learn many things about angels. However, we will only encounter them when they serve some specific purpose in the plan and program of God. Therefore, while there are many things that we may want to know about them, the Bible will only tell us what we need to know.

SUMMARY TO QUESTION 1
DO ANGELS ACTUALLY EXIST?

Scripture teaches there are other rational personal beings which exist in the universe that are distinct from God and humans. The Bible calls one group of them angels.

From the first book of the Bible, until the last, the existence of angels is clearly taught in hundreds of different references. Angels are always assumed to have genuine existence; they are never treated as mythical characters.

In addition to the overall testimony of Scripture, we also have the clear teaching of Jesus on the subject; He believed in angels. Since He is God the Son, His Word settles the issue. Therefore, we conclude that angels truly do exist.

While angels do exist, our knowledge about them is limited since they are not the central characters in Scripture. Indeed, the Bible is all about

God and His dealings with the human race. The subject of angels is only secondary to the main story.

Consequently these spirit-beings only appear in the Bible when their actions have something to do with the central theme; God and His dealings with humanity.

Since our knowledge will always be incomplete we must realize that there will be certain things about angels that we do not know because God has not told us.

Therefore, when we investigate this subject we must realize the limitations of our study. In other words, there is much to learn about these personages, but there will also be many questions which will remain unanswered.

QUESTION 2

Who Are Angels?

Angels are God's messengers. They are spirit-beings who have been specifically created to do the work of the Lord. The Bible says their nature is one of "spirit." We read the following in the Book of Hebrews.

> And of the angels He says: "Who makes His angels spirits And His ministers a flame of fire" (Hebrews 1:7 NKJV).

The writer to the Hebrews also said.

> Are they not all ministering spirits sent forth to minister for those who will inherit salvation? (Hebrews 1:14 NKJV).

Angels are ministering spirits who were created to do the work of the Lord. In particular, they are to minister to the believers¬; those who will inherit God's salvation.

This definition is important to keep in mind for we will discover other heavenly beings that the Lord has created, who are not called angels, and who are never sent to do His bidding. They include the "living creatures" the "cherubim" and "seraphim." We will answer specific questions about these created beings later in this book.

ANGELS IN THE OLD TESTAMENT

The Hebrew word translated "angel" is *mal'ak*. This term, used 103 times in the Old Testament, simply means "messenger." It refers to one who brings a message in the place of another person. The term is mainly used of heavenly messengers. For example, we read the following description about them in Jacob's famous dream.

> He had a dream in which he saw a stairway resting on the earth, with its top reaching to heaven, and the angels of God were ascending and descending on it (Genesis 28:12 NIV).

In Jacob's dream, he saw a "stairway to heaven" from the earth. On this stairway were the angels, God's messengers, coming and going.

THE HEBREW WORD IS USED OF HUMANS IN THE OLD TESTAMENT

However, the term is also used of earthly messengers; such as Haggai the prophet, and a priest in the Book of Malachi.

We read in Haggai.

> Then Haggai, the messenger of the Lord, spoke to the people with the Lord's message, "I am with you, declares the Lord (Haggai 1:13 ESV).

In this case, the "angel," or messenger, was a prophet of God, Haggai, not a heavenly being.

Malachi used the Hebrew term to refer to priests.

> For the lips of a priest ought to preserve knowledge, and from his mouth men should seek instruction—because he is the messenger of the LORD Almighty (Malachi 2:7 NIV).

In these instances, the Hebrew word for angel is translated as messenger, because human messengers were in view. The context usually makes it clear. However, in some cases, it is difficult to tell whether the Bible is speaking about an earthly or a heavenly messenger.

Interestingly, in the Old Testament section of the "prophets," the plural form of the word is more often used of earthly messengers rather than heavenly messengers. Again, the context should always be used to determine whether an earthly being, or a heavenly being, is in mind.

ANGELS IN THE NEW TESTAMENT

In the New Testament, the Greek word *angelos*, translated "angel," likewise means, "messenger." As we can readily see, our English word "angel" is derived from this Greek term *angelos*.

The term "angel" has the idea of someone who speaks or acts in the place of the one who sent him. It is used one hundred and seventy-five times in the New Testament—the great majority of the time it refers to heavenly messengers.

THE WORD ALSO REFERS TO HUMANS MESSENGERS IN SOME CONTEXTS

However, on six occasions in the New Testament, the term angel refers to human beings. Jesus said to the multitudes about John the Baptist.

> John is the one about whom Scripture says, 'I'm sending my messenger ahead of you to prepare the way in front of you' (Matthew 11:10 God's Word).

Mark wrote the Lord sending His messenger to the people.

> As it is written in the Prophets: "Behold, I send My messenger before Your face, Who will prepare Your way before You" (Mark 1:2 NKJV).

In these two instances, the word messenger is a translation the Greek word *angelos*, angel.

Luke used the Greek term "angels" to refer to the messengers of John the Baptist.

> After John's messengers left, Jesus began to speak to the crowd about John: "What did you go out into the desert to see? A reed swayed by the wind?" (Luke 7:24 NIV).

He also used it to refer to John the Baptist.

> John is the man to whom the Scriptures refer when they say,
> 'Look, I am sending my messenger before you, and he will
> prepare your way before you' (Luke 7:27 NLT).

Luke later used this term to refer to messengers that Jesus sent ahead to
Samaria. We read the following statement.

> He sent messengers ahead of Him, and on the way they
> entered a village of the Samaritans to make preparations for
> Him (Luke 9:52 HCSB).

Again, in each of these instances, the Greek word *angelos* is used and is
translated "messenger" or "messengers."

James uses this Greek word to describe the spies that Rahab the prostitute hid from the people of Jericho. He wrote.

> Likewise, was not Rahab the harlot also justified by works
> when she received the messengers and sent them out another
> way? (James 2:25 NKJV).

Therefore, we have a number of references in the New Testament where
the Greek word *angelos* is translated as messenger, since it is referring to
human messengers, not heavenly ones.

THE MESSENGER OF SATAN TORMENTED PAUL

In another use of the term, the Apostle Paul used the phrase "messenger
[angel] of Satan" when referring to some personal problem that he had.

> Therefore, in order to keep me from becoming conceited, I
> was given a thorn in my flesh, a messenger of Satan, to tor-
> ment me (2 Corinthians 12:7 NIV).

Consequently, while the Greek word speaks primarily of "spirit beings" there are seven instances in the New Testament where it refers to something else.

THE BIBLE SPEAKS OF "ANGELS OF HEAVEN"

Often we find in the New Testament qualifying phrases such as "angels of heaven" (Matthew 24:36) when referring to angelic creatures. Phrases like this make it clear that angelic personages are in view. The context usually makes it clear whether we are dealing with earthly or heavenly messengers.

SUMMARY TO QUESTION 2
WHO ARE ANGELS?

The Bible says that angels are invisible, personal spirit-beings who have been created by God. Simply stated, they are His "messengers."

The Hebrew word, as well as the Greek word, translated "angel," simply means messenger. It refers to someone who has the authority to relay a message from the person who sent them.

Therefore, these spirit-beings have a specific purpose, they are God's messengers. In other words, they do His bidding since they have been sent by Him.

While the Hebrew and Greek words which are translated "angel" usually refer to these spirit beings, on several occasions in the New Testament they are used to describe human messengers. On one occasion the word is used to describe Paul's "thorn in the flesh." He described it as a "messenger of Satan."

The Hebrew word, likewise, refers to human messengers in many contexts. In fact, the plural form of the word, when used in the section of the Old Testament prophets, mostly refers to human messengers, not heavenly ones. Therefore, it is important that the context inform us exactly what type of messenger is in view.

Finally, we need to make the distinction between angels and other heavenly beings. Scripture speaks of these personages known as the "living creatures," the "seraphim" and "cherubim." They are always kept distinct from angels. Indeed, they are described differently, as well as having a different function than the angels. Therefore, it would be a mistake to classify them as such.

QUESTION 3

What Do We Know About Angels From The Bible?

Our concern in this book is with the heavenly creatures called "angels." What do we know about them? What does the Bible tell us? From Scripture we learn a number of important things.

1. THEY ARE CREATED BEINGS

To begin with, we find that angels are created beings—they have not existed eternally. Though the Genesis creation account does not record the creation of angels, we know from other passages that they were directly made by the power of God Almighty. The psalmist speaks of the creation of angels.

> Praise him, all his angels; praise him, all his hosts! For he commanded and they were created. And he established them forever and ever; he gave a decree, and it shall not pass away (Psalm 148:2,5,6 ESV).

The Lord made the celestial bodies, as well as the angels, by His spoken Word, the command of God!

In the Book of Ezra, we find that the Lord created all that there is in the universe.

> You alone are the Lord. You made the heavens, even the highest heavens, and all their starry host, the earth and all

21

that is on it, the seas and all that is in them. You give life to everything, and the multitudes of heaven worship you (Nehemiah 9:6 ESV).

"All that is on it" would include the angels. The phrase "host of heaven" probably refers to the creation of angels as well as other heavenly beings such as the living creatures, the cherubim and seraphim.

2. THEY WERE CREATED BY JESUS CHRIST

The Bible says that Jesus Christ created all things, visible and invisible. Paul wrote the following to the Colossians.

Christ is the one through whom God created everything in heaven and earth. He made the things we can see and the things we can't see— kings, kingdoms, rulers, and authorities. Everything has been created through him and for him (Colossians 1:16 NLT).

Specifically mentioned in the things that Christ created are thrones, dominions, rulers, and powers. These are terms that seem to refer to ranks of angels. They also likely refer to other heavenly beings that the Lord has created.

3. THEY ARE DEPENDENT CREATURES

Because the angels have been created, they are dependent creatures— they need God to exist. Like humanity, they have no independent existence apart from God. God is the only being who is, by nature, self-existent—He needs nothing else to exist.

Paul wrote about creatures which are not God.

Formerly, when you did not know God, you were slaves to those who by nature are not gods (Galatians 4:8 NIV).

Only the Lord is God by nature, everything else is created. This includes angels as well as all other spirit-beings.

4. THEY ARE A SEPARATE CREATION FROM HUMANITY

Angels are a different type of creation than humans. In fact, we have nothing in common with them in our physical nature that binds us together. Though all humans are racially bound together, we are distinct from the angels. Even in our resurrection bodies we will not become angels.

5. THEY WERE CREATED ABOVE HUMANS

The Bible teaches that angels are a distinct created order above humanity. The Scripture says.

> You made him lower than the angels for a short time; You crowned him with glory and honor (Hebrews 2:7 HCSB).

Humans are the highest creation that the Lord has made here on the earth. Indeed, we have been created above the entire animal kingdom. Angels are one of God's creations in heaven. However, exactly how they fit in with the other heavenly beings in order of importance is not revealed to us.

6. THEY ARE NOT A RACE

Angels are a company of beings rather than a race. They do not marry, neither are they male or female. They are sexless, unmarriageable, creatures who do not propagate their own kind. Jesus said the following about humans in the heavenly realm.

> For in the resurrection they neither marry nor are given in marriage, but are like angels in heaven (Matthew 22:30 ESV).

This is important to understand. They are not a race like humans.

7. THEY ARE INVISIBLE SPIRIT BEINGS

Angels are spirit beings who are invisible to the human eye.

In speaking of the angels he says, "He makes his angels spirits, and his servants flames of fire" (Hebrews 1:7 NIV).

By nature, they have no physical form, at least not like our human bodies. Jesus made this point when referring to His resurrection body. He
said the following to His disciples.

> See my hands and my feet, that it is I myself. Touch me, and
> see. For a spirit does not have flesh and bones as you see that
> I have (Luke 24:39 ESV).

Their spirit-form does not necessarily imply that they have no body
at all, merely that it is not a human body of flesh and bones. In other
words, they have a different makeup from humanity.

Whether angels are pure spirit, such as God, or have some type of
material existence, such as humans, is a much debated point. Like so
many issues dealing with this subject, the Bible does not comment on
it. What we can safely say is that angels do not have any form, or sub-
stance, like humans. Beyond this it is only speculation.

8. THEY HAVE AN ANGELIC NATURE

Angels have their own unique nature. The spirit-nature of angels is not
the same as God's spirit nature, or our human nature. God's nature, or
essence, is that of spirit. Jesus said.

> God is Spirit, and those who worship Him must worship in
> spirit and truth (John 4:24 NKJV).

We must keep in mind that God is an uncreated Spirit—a Being that
has always existed. Angels are created, invisible, spirit-beings. Humans
and angels will keep their distinction in the ages to come. Humans will
not become angels, and angels will not become human.

9. THEY ARE NOT SUBJECT TO NATURAL LAW

Therefore angels, as spirit-creatures, are not limited to physical or natural conditions. They are not subject to the laws of nature. Angels can

pass back and forth from the spiritual realm to the natural realm. In the Book of Acts we read.

> And behold, an angel of the Lord stood next to him, and a light shone in the cell. He struck Peter on the side and woke him, saying, "Get up quickly." And the chains fell off his hands (Acts 12:7 ESV).

The angel "appeared" in the cell where Simon Peter was jailed. Physical boundaries present no obstacles for these angelic creatures.

10. THEY CAN ASSUME A HUMAN BODY

Though they have no physical form, angels can, at times, assume a body as the Lord allows them. This is known as an "angelophany"—the appearance of an angel.

For example, an angel rolled the stone away from the tomb of Jesus, and then proceed to sit upon it.

> There was a violent earthquake, for an angel of the Lord came down from heaven and, going to the tomb, rolled back the stone and sat on it (Matthew 28:2 NIV).

Thus, angels are unseen by humans until God chooses a time when they are to appear. We cannot be exactly certain whether the bodies these angels assumed were real bodies, or only appeared to be real. There is not enough information to know for certain.

We do know that angels are capable of materializing only when God wills, In other words, they cannot do something like this on their own.

On one occasion we find them eating. Three angels, who appeared as men, visited Abraham. The Bible then describes these angels eating the food which Abraham has prepared.

> When the food was ready, he took some cheese curds and milk and the roasted meat, and he served it to the men. As

they ate, Abraham waited on them there beneath the trees (Genesis 18:8 NLT).

This indicates, at least for that one episode, the angels took on a real body, and with it, were able to eat.

11. THEY ALWAYS APPEAR AS MEN

When angels have appeared to humans in biblical times, their appearance is always that of a man, either a young man or an older one. Indeed, on a number of occasions angels were described in Scripture as men. We find this happening to the prophets Ezekiel, Daniel and Zechariah.

> When he brought me there, behold, there was a man whose appearance was like bronze, with a linen cord and a measuring reed in his hand. And he was standing in the gateway (Ezekiel 40:3 ESV).

> Again one having the appearance of a man touched me and strengthened me And he said, "O man greatly loved, fear not, peace be with you; be strong and of good courage." And as he spoke to me, I was strengthened and said, "Let my lord speak, for you have strengthened me" (Daniel 10: 18,19 ESV).

> When I looked again, I saw a man with a measuring line in his hand. "Where are you going?" I asked. He replied, "I am going to measure Jerusalem, to see how wide and how long it is (Zechariah 2:1 NLT).

In each of these instances these men were soon, if not immediately, recognized as spirit-beings, and not mere mortals.

However, on other occasions, angels were immediately recognized as angels. For example, we read the following experience of the Gentile prophet Balaam.

26

Then the Lord opened Balaam's eyes, and he saw the angel of the Lord standing in the roadway with a drawn sword in his hand. Balaam bowed his head and fell face down on the ground before him (Numbers 22:31 NLT).

Like Balaam, David immediately recognized an angel when he appeared.

When David saw the angel, he said to the Lord, "I am the one who has sinned and done wrong! But these people are as innocent as sheep—what have they done? Let your anger fall against me and my family" (2 Samuel 24:17 NLT).

Zechariah, the father of John the Baptist, was greeted by an angel.

And there appeared to him an angel of the Lord standing on the right side of the altar of incense. And Zechariah was troubled when he saw him, and fear fell upon him (Luke 1:11-12 ESV).

He became fearful when he realized that an angel had appeared to him.

Mary, the mother of Jesus, was visited by the same angel, Gabriel.

In the sixth month the angel Gabriel was sent from God to a city of Galilee named Nazareth, to a virgin betrothed to a man whose name was Joseph, of the house of David. And the virgin's name was Mary. And he came to her and said, "Greetings, O favored one, the Lord is with you!" But she was greatly troubled at the saying, and tried to discern what sort of greeting this might be (Luke 1:26-29 ESV).

As we can observe, in each of these appearances the angels were immediately recognized as angels.

12. THEY ARE ABLE TO MOVE RAPIDLY

Scripture tells us that angels can move rapidly. They are represented as flying in the Book of Revelation. The Bible says.

> Then I saw another angel flying high overhead, having the eternal gospel to announce to the inhabitants of the earth—to every nation, tribe, language, and people (Revelation 14:6 HCSB).

The fact that they are represented as flying gave rise to the notion that they have wings. However, wings for flight apply to beings that function in our world. Angels do not need wings to move rapidly in the unseen world.

Two distinct types of heavenly beings, the cherubim and seraphim, are represented as having wings. However, the angels which have appeared to humans are *never* described as having wings.

13. THEY ARE NUMEROUS

The Scripture teaches that the number of angels is very great. This is expressed in various ways. We read the following in the Book of Psalms.

> The chariots of God are tens of thousands and thousands of thousands; the Lord has come from Sinai into his sanctuary (Psalm 68:17 NIV).

The "chariots of God" is a term referring to angels. They are described here as numerous.

We find that Daniel saw an innumerable amount of angels before God's throne. We read.

> A river of fire was flowing, coming out from before him. Thousands upon thousands attended him; ten thousand times ten thousand stood before him. The court was seated, and the books were opened (Daniel 7:10 NIV).

Again, we find a huge number of angels mentioned. Since this is speaking of beings around the throne of God, it also likely refers to other heavenly beings which the Lord has created.

At the birth of Jesus, armies of angels appeared. Luke tells us the following took place

> Suddenly, the angel was joined by a vast host of others—the armies of heaven—praising God (Luke 2:13 NLT).

A "vast host" speaks of countless numbers.

When Jesus was betrayed by Judas Iscariot in the Garden of Gethsemane, Christ told His disciples that He could command more than twelve legions of angels to appear and protect Him.

> Or do you think that I cannot call on My Father, and He will provide Me at once with more than 12 legions of angels? (Matthew 26:53 HCSB).

A legion consisted of about three to five thousand men. Twelve legions of angels would have been a way of saying an extremely large number of angels were at His disposal. The New Living Translations says.

> Don't you realize that I could ask my Father for thousands of angels to protect us, and he would send them instantly? (Matthew 26:53 NLT).

In sum, Jesus had numerous angels at His disposal.

In the Book of Hebrews, the Bible also speaks of innumerable angels.

> But you have come to Mount Zion and to the city of the living God, the heavenly Jerusalem, and to innumerable angels in festal gathering (Hebrews 12:22 NRSV).

We also find that the Book of Revelation speaks of the countless number of angels.

> Then I looked, and I heard the voice of many angels around
> the throne, the living creatures, and the elders; and the num-
> ber of them was ten thousand times ten thousand, and thou-
> sands of thousands (Revelation 5:11 NKJV).

If this number were to be taken literally, it would be two hundred million! Whatever the case may be, the Bible testifies that there are many
angels that exist.

However, we should note that the Bible here distinguishes between the
elders, which number twenty-four, the angels, and the living creatures.
Each is a distinct group.

14. THERE ARE A LIMITED NUMBER OF THEM

Though numerous, the exact number of angels is finite. Since they
cannot bear children, angels cannot, by themselves, bring other angels
into existence.

Scripture also indicates that all the angels have already been created—
the creation of angels does not now happen, and seemingly, never will
again.

We read the following words in Colossians.

> For in him all things were created: things in heaven and on
> earth, visible and invisible, whether thrones or powers or rul-
> ers or authorities; all things have been created through him
> and for him (Colossians 1:16 NIV).

The Bible also tells us that God has ceased creating anything new; this
includes angels. We read about this in the second chapter of the Book
of Genesis.

> Thus the heavens and the earth, and all the host of them,
> were finished. And on the seventh day God ended His work
> which He had done, and He rested on the seventh day from
> all His work which He had done (Genesis 2:1,2 NKJV).

The "host of heaven" is another designation for angels as well as other heavenly beings which the Lord has created.

15. THEY ARE IMMORTAL

Angels are not subject to death—they are immortal. Their immortality has been given to them by God, who Himself is immortal by nature. Paul wrote the following about the nature of God.

> The only One who has immortality, dwelling in unapproachable light; no one has seen or can see Him, to Him be honor and eternal might. Amen (1 Timothy 6:16 HCSB).

Angels do not possess immortality in and of themselves. Like humans, their immortality is derived from God. Jesus told the Sadducees that resurrected believers would be like angels—they would never die.

> For they cannot die anymore, because they are equal to angels and are sons of God, being sons of the resurrection (Luke 20:36 ESV).

Death is something that humanity has experienced because of sin. Since these righteous angels did not sin, they will not experience death. Because they are beings that do not possess human bodies, they do not understand either growth or death. The number of angels, therefore, cannot decrease.

16. THEY ARE PERSONAL BEINGS

Angels are personal beings—they can be interacted with. They have every feature of personality such as intelligence, thought, and choice. We know that at least two of the angels, Michael and Gabriel, have personal names.

> The Bible says that angels have desired to look into the glorious things of salvation. It was revealed to them that they were serving not themselves but you, in regard to

the things that have now been announced to you through those who brought you good news by the Holy Spirit sent from heaven—things into which angels long to look! (1 Peter 1:12 NRSV).

This desire on their part is a sign of personality. The personality of angels can further be seen by the fact that they have powers of speech, memory, and the ability to ask and answer questions. Like humanity, angels were created with choice.

The fact that there were some angels who decided to rebel against God demonstrates that each of them could choose whom they would serve. This is a further example that God made the angels as personal beings.

This briefly sums up what the Scripture says about angels, God's invisible messengers. While there is much that we learn about them from the Bible there are many things that are not revealed.

SUMMARY TO QUESTION 3
WHAT DO WE KNOW ABOUT ANGELS FROM THE BIBLE?

Angels are majestic spirit-beings whom the Lord has created to execute His divine will for time and eternity. While angels are not the main characters of Scripture, we do know a number of things about them from the Bible.

To begin with, they are created beings, they have not existed eternally. At a certain point in time the Lord brought them into existence. Jesus Christ, God the Son, was involved in the creation of angels.

Because angels are created beings they are dependent creatures. In other words, like the human race, they need God for their continued existence. However, they were created as a higher order of being than the human race.

Angels should be considered as a different order of being than humans in the sense that their number cannot increase or decrease. They do not marry or have children. While numerous, there is a finite number of them.

Angels have their own unique nature that is invisible to the human eye. Unless the Lord allows them to be seen, they remain unseen by humans. Consequently, we only know about them through God's divine revelation to us, the Bible.

Scripture describes them as beings which are not subject to natural law. They are able to easily move from the invisible dimension to the visible one.

At times, they have assumed a human body for a short period of time. In doing so, they always appear as men.

They are personal beings. In fact two of the angels are named for us, Michael and Gabriel.

This sums up some of the basic facts which the Bible reveals about angels.

QUESTION 4

What Do We Learn About Angels From The Everyday Speech Of People In Biblical Times?

While the Bible directly teaches us a number of things about angels, we can also learn much about them from the way people spoke of them in their ordinary speech.

Indeed, when people in biblical times spoke of angels they often referred to their supernatural qualities and abilities. We have a number of examples in Scripture where the everyday speech of the people gives us insight into how they viewed angels.

ANGELS WERE VIEWED AS BEING TRUSTWORTHY

For example, David had defected to the side of the Philistines. After being with them for a period of time, King Achish said to him

> I am convinced that you are as reliable as the angel of God (1 Samuel 29: 9 NET).

This pagan king compared David's behavior to that of an angel. In other words, David could be counted upon to be trustworthy. Therefore, angels were viewed as beings who were trustworthy, those who could be relied upon.

ANGELS HAD SUPERIOR WISDOM TO HUMANS

There is also the account of a wise woman from Tekoa who approached King David in disguise. In speaking to him, she spoke of the superior wisdom of angels.

> And now your servant says, 'May the word of my lord the king secure my inheritance, for my lord the king is like an angel of God in discerning good and evil' (2 Samuel 14:17 NIV).

In this instance, we discover that the people viewed angels as beings who had a superior ability to discern right from wrong.

When King David asked the woman whether Joab was the one who plotted against him, she replied as follows.

> Yes, it was your servant Joab who instructed me to do this and who put all these words into the mouth of your servant. Your servant Joab did this to change the present situation. My lord has wisdom like that of an angel of God—he knows everything that happens in the land (2 Samuel 14:19,20 NIV).

Again we have the emphasis that angels have superior wisdom to humans.

ANGELS WERE WORTHY OF SPECIAL RESPECT

When Paul wrote to the Galatians, he recalled the former kindness that the people had shown to him.

> As you know, it was because of an illness that I first preached the gospel to you, and even though my illness was a trial to you, you did not treat me with contempt or scorn. Instead, you welcomed me as if I were an angel of God, as if I were Christ Jesus himself (Galatians 4:14 NIV).

They treated Paul in a special way, the same way they would welcome an angel of God. In other words, while they were not to be worshipped, angels were worthy of very special respect.

PAUL WROTE OF THE ELOQUENCE OF THE LANGUAGE WHICH ANGELS SPEAK

In his great section on love, Paul wrote to the Corinthians about the eloquence of angels.

> If I speak in the tongues of men and of angels, but I do not have love, I am a noisy gong or a clanging cymbal (1 Corinthians 13:1 NET).

Evidently, angels were viewed as having superior eloquence to humans.

ANGELS ARE PRESENTLY SUPERIOR TO HUMANS

When Jesus refuted the arguments of the Sadducees against angels and their view of the resurrection of the dead, He pointed out the present superiority of angels to human beings. The Lord said.

> The people of this age marry and are given in marriage. But those who are considered worthy of taking part in the age to come and in the resurrection from the dead will neither marry nor be given in marriage, and they can no longer die; for they are like the angels. They are God's children, since they are children of the resurrection (Luke 20:34-36 NIV).

This is consistent with what we find elsewhere in Scripture. Those who are "worthy" to take part in the coming age will have a position similar to the righteous angels. This indicates that angels are presently viewed as being superior beings to humans.

37

GOD THE SON, IN HIS HUMANITY, WAS LOWER IN POSITION THAN THE ANGELS

This is confirmed by what the Scripture teaches about Jesus coming into our world. When Jesus, God the Son, was here upon the earth, He humbled Himself as a human being. In fact, the writer of Hebrews, stated that Christ temporarily assumed a position which was inferior to that of the angels.

> What we do see is Jesus, who was given a position "a little lower than the angels"; and because he suffered death for us, he is now "crowned with glory and honor (Hebrews 2:9 NET).

While Jesus was superior in His nature to angels, He took a position of inferiority to the angels when He became a human being. However, as the writer stated, Christ ultimately will be the supreme ruler over everything, including angels. Indeed, He is now crowned with glory and honor.

From these passages, we learn much about how angels were generally viewed by the people in biblical times. In their everyday speech we discover that angels were seen as trustworthy beings, who were superior to humans in their wisdom. In fact, when God the Son became a human being, He humbled Himself, taking a position inferior to that of angels.

SUMMARY TO QUESTION 4
WHAT DO WE LEARN ABOUT ANGELS FROM THE EVERYDAY SPEECH OF PEOPLE IN BIBLICAL TIMES?

From the everyday speech of people in biblical times, it is possible to discover how angels were viewed. In fact, the Bible gives us a number of instances where people, in their normal conversation, revealed how angels were perceived by them.

We discover that angels were always viewed as superior beings to humans. In fact, they had wisdom and knowledge above ours. While angels do occupy a superior position to humans, this will not always be true. Those who have believed in the God of the Bible will be given a superior position to angels in the world to come.

Furthermore, Scripture says that God the Son, Jesus Christ, in becoming a human took a position of inferiority to the angels. Of course, this position was only temporary. He has now been crowned with glory and honor and He will rule over everything, including angels.

QUESTION 5

Why Should We Take The Time To Study About Angels?

We have found that angels do exist. However, we have also discovered that they are not the central characters of Scripture. In fact, they are only mentioned when they have something to do with the plan and program of God. Otherwise, the Bible gives us no further information about them.

This being the case, then why should anyone take their time to study about angels? Of what benefit can it be to look into this subject? We can list a number of reasons why this is so.

REASON 1: THE SUBJECT OF ANGELS IS CONTAINED GOD'S WORD

To begin with, the subject of angels is contained in the Scripture and we are told that everything found in the Bible if profitable for our study. In fact, this is the testimony of Scripture. Paul wrote.

> Everything in the Scriptures is God's Word. All of it is useful for teaching and helping people and for correcting them and showing them how to live. The Scriptures train God's servants to do all kinds of good deeds (2 Timothy 3:16,17 CEV).

The New International Version puts it this way.

> All Scripture is God-breathed and is useful for teaching, rebuking, correcting and training in righteousness, so that

the servant of God may be thoroughly equipped for every good work (2 Timothy 3:16,17 NIV).

Everything that contained in Scripture is useful for us. Therefore, since the subject of angels is taught in the Word of God, it is important that Christians understand what the Bible has to say about it.

REASON 2: ANGELS ARE PROMINENT IN SCRIPTURE

One of the main reasons for the study of angels is their prominence in Scripture. While not the main characters in the biblical story, they still are mentioned frequently.

In fact, there is much said about angels and their function. Their influence is not restricted to any one time in history. Indeed, we find angels being involved in the work of God from Genesis to Revelation. Since the Bible gives much space to their ministry, we ought to pay attention to what Scripture says about them.

REASON 3: THEY PLAY AN IMPORTANT FUNCTION IN GOD'S PLAN

Furthermore, their function is important for us to understand. Since they play an important role in God's overall plan for humanity, it is necessary for us to understand the extent of their involvement and how they relate to us.

In doing so, it will help us to further understand what the Lord has done in the past, what He is now doing, as well as what He will do in the future. Angels play a big part in His program.

REASON 4: THEY WILL EXIST FOREVER ALONGSIDE HUMANS

We are also told that the righteous angels and the believing humans will exist together forever. This alone is a good reason to get acquainted with them.

REASON 5: THEY REMIND US THE UNSEEN WORLD IS REAL

Add to this, a study of angels reminds us that the unseen world is real. It informs us that we are not the only beings in the universe. There are unseen forces, both good and evil, that are all around us. These forces are in a constant spiritual battle.

REASON 6: WE NEED TO CLEAR UP IGNORANCE ON THIS SUBJECT

In addition, a study of the subject of angels from the Scripture will clear up ignorance on the subject. Are these spirit-beings friendly or hostile? Do they cause us harm? Since angels live beyond our means of detection, we need a reliable source that will give us the correct answers to these questions.

The Bible is the final authority on all matters of faith and practice. In other words, whatever it says about the subject of angels is the final word on the matter. Thus, we can know for certain who angels are, and what they do, because we have an authoritative source that tells us so.

REASON 7: THEY ENCOURAGE CONSISTENT LIVING FROM BELIEVERS

The study of angels should encourage believers to live consistent Christian lives, seeing they are observing our every move. Paul wrote the following.

> For I think that God has displayed us, the apostles, last, as men condemned to death; for we have been made a spectacle to the world, both to angels and to men (1 Corinthians 4:9 NKJV).

The New Living Translation says.

> But sometimes I think God has put us apostles on display, like prisoners of war at the end of a victor's parade, condemned to die. We have become a spectacle to the entire world— to people and angels alike (1 Corinthians 4:9 NLT).

Seemingly everything that we do is observed by angels. If believers realize this truth, then it should further encourage us to live consistently with our beliefs.

Of course, whether angels can see us or not, we know that God always sees everything that we do! That should be the main motivation to live a life that is pleasing to Him.

REASON 8: WE WILL BE CONFIDENT IN GOD'S PROTECTION OF US

Angels also serve a protective function for the believer in Jesus Christ. The Bible says.

> For he will command his angels concerning you to guard you in all your ways; they will lift you up in their hands, so that you will not strike your foot against a stone (Psalm 91:11,12 NIV).

Our faith in God's providential care is strengthened when we understand the ministry of angels. Since God has placed these intelligent creatures to guide and protect believers, it will strengthen our faith in Him and His concern for us.

REASON 9: WE CAN LEARN FROM THEIR EXAMPLE

Angels also provide examples for believers as to how we should live. They are continually in worship and service to God. Believers should learn to imitate that behavior.

Jesus told us to pray in this manner.

> Your kingdom come. Your will be done, on earth as it is in heaven (Matthew 6:10 NRSV).

God's will is being accomplished in heaven through the ministry of angels. They do His bidding continually, joyfully, and with unquestioned obedience. Believers should learn to do likewise.

In sum, there are a number of important reasons as to why we should study the subject of angels.

SUMMARY TO QUESTION 5
WHY SHOULD WE TAKE THE TIME TO STUDY ABOUT ANGELS?

Though angels are not the main characters of the Bible, the study of the their ministry can be profitable for a number of reasons. They can be summed up as follows.

First, the doctrine of angels is part of Holy Scripture. Since we are told that all Scripture is profitable for us to study, this would include the teachings we find about angels. Therefore, doing a study on the subject of angels should bring great benefit to the believer.

In addition, while not the main theme of the Bible, angels certainly play a prominent role in Scripture. So much is said about them by the writers of the Bible that it should encourage us to understand who they are, and what they do.

Indeed, they have an important function in the overall plan of God as well as in the lives of believers. Therefore, a study of them is profitable.

In fact, we will not know anything about their involvement unless we study the Scriptures. If we are to understand the complete plan of God for time and eternity, then the study of angels is necessary.

Furthermore, a study of angels reminds us of the reality of the unseen world. There is a world that exists which is unseen to the human eye. Angels are a big part of this world. Studying about angels will constantly remind us of this.

Understanding what the Bible says about angels will also clear up ignorance on the subject, a subject in which there is unfortunately much ignorance.

Realizing that angels are observing us should encourage us to live more godly lives. Scripture says they are watching our every move. Of course, we also know that the Lord knows everything we do as well as everything that we think. Pleasing Him should be our primary motivation.

Understanding that angels protect believers will comfort us in times of trouble. This should be very encouraging. We are being looked after! Angels are a big part of the protection that the Lord provides for us.

We also have their example of devoted service to God. Their continual service to the Lord should be a challenge to us to behave in the same manner.

Consequently the study of angels will have many benefits.

QUESTION 6

Why Are There So Many
Misconceptions About Angels?

The study of angels can bring great benefits. Among them is the clearing up of misconceptions that people hold about them. Unfortunately, the misconceptions are many. Why is this so? Why do people seem to have so many wrong ideas about angels?

The reasons for certain misconceptions about angels can be attributed to the following.

1. THERE IS THE REJECTION OF THE SUPERNATURAL

Often the subject of angels is ignored or misunderstood because of the rejection of the supernatural. Since the existence of God is rejected, the existence of angels is likewise rejected. Those who do not accept the Bible as God's Word are not going to turn to Scripture to discover anything about angels. They assume that angels do not exist. Therefore, they go through life with the misconception that angels, as the Bible portrays them, are mythical creatures.

2. THERE IS IGNORANCE OF SCRIPTURE

Ignorance of what the Bible says on the subject of angels also leads to misconceptions. Though many people may accept the fact that angels do indeed exist, they have not turned to the Scripture to find out who they are, and what they can and cannot do. Personal experiences and fanciful stories replace what God has said on the subject. This leads to a variety of misconceptions about these angelic beings.

3. THERE IS SUPERSTITION AND FEAR OF THE UNKNOWN

Consequently the subject of angels is often treated with superstition and fear. This can lead to all types of strange beliefs and behavior with respect to angels. People can give undue adoration, prayer, and even worship to these created spiritual beings.

The remedy for these problems is simple: one must turn to the pages of Scripture to discover what God has to say on the subject rather than looking to other sources of information on these heavenly beings.

The Bible encourages people to study the Scriptures and test the spirits. Paul wrote.

> Test all things; hold fast what is good (1 Thessalonians 5:21 NKJV).

John declared that we are to test the spirits. He said.

> Dear friends, don't believe all people who say that they have the Spirit. Instead, test them. See whether the spirit they have is from God, because there are many false prophets in the world (1 John 4:1 God's Word).

Therefore a careful study of the Word of God will clear up these and other misconceptions about angels.

In sum, there is no reason for any of us to have misconceptions about angels. Indeed, the true facts about them are found in the pages of the Bible.

SUMMARY TO QUESTION 6
WHY ARE THERE SO MANY MISCONCEPTIONS ABOUT ANGELS?

Unhappily, many times the subject of angels is approached with a number of misconceptions. They include the following.

One common misconception is the rejection of the supernatural. If people deny the supernatural exists, then certainly they will deny the reality of angels. Consequently, the subject of angels is never even considered by the unbeliever.

There is also ignorance of Scripture. Those who take the Bible seriously must admit the existence of angels. Angels are part of the biblical story from the beginning to the end. However, too many believers do not take the time to read and study the Bible. This being the case, they will be ignorant with respect to what the Bible has to say on the subject.

Indeed, since Jesus believed in angels, then we must believe in them also. Unfortunately many people are unaware of Jesus' belief in angels.

There is also much superstition and fear about angels which also contributes misconceptions to this subject. People often are convinced of certain realities about angels which have no real basis in fact. Again, this occurs when they do not go to the one source that accurately tells us what we need to know about angels, the Bible.

In fact, all of these misconceptions are associated with not taking seriously what the Bible has to say.

However once someone takes the time to consider what the Bible teaches on the subject, the denial of angels, as well as ignorance and fear concerning them, will disappear. These misconceptions come from a lack of study of what the Scripture says.

QUESTION 7

When Were
Angels Created?

Angels are created beings. They have been made for the purpose of doing the bidding of God. We will now see what the Bible has to say with respect to their creation.

1. THEY WERE CREATED AT THE BEGINNING

The first verse of Scripture gives us an indication as to when the angels were created. It says the following.

> In the beginning God created the heavens and the earth (Genesis 1:1 KJV).

The phrase "heavens and the earth" refers to the entire universe. This would include all the separate parts. While the creation of angels could possibly be included in this statement, this is not necessarily true. In fact, this may be ruled out when we consider our next point.

2. THEY WERE PROBABLY CREATED BEFORE THE EARTH WAS CREATED

Though we are not told exactly when they were created, it seems to be sometime before the earth was created. God spoke to Job saying.

> Where were you when I laid the foundation of the earth? Tell me if you have such insight. Who determined its dimensions? Certainly, you know! Who stretched a measuring line

over it? On what were its footings sunk? Who laid its corner-
stone when the morning stars sang together and all the sons
of God shouted for joy? (Job 38:4-7 God's Word).

The term "sons of God" may be one of the many designations for
angels, as the Book of Job earlier states.

One day the sons of God came to present themselves before
the Lord, and Satan also came with them (Job 1:6 HCSB).

If the phrase "sons of God" is referring to angels in Job 38, then when
God created the heavens and the earth, the angels had already been in
existence, likely for some time.

Therefore, if this is a literal description of what happened in the beginning, then angels were around long before the universe was created.

There is something else we learn from this passage in Job 38, if it is
a literal description of what took place at the beginning. The phrase
"sons of God" in this context refers to righteous angels. We know that
all angels are not righteous now. Indeed, there are a number of fallen
angels led by the devil.

So either this is a statement of all the angels praising God when He
created the universe, which would mean that it took place before some
fell into sin, or it would indicate that God's creation of the universe
happened after the angelic rebellion. In this case, it would be only the
angels who stayed faithful to the Lord that praised Him.

There is one more thing that we should mention. The phrase "sons of
God" in this context may refer to some of the other heavenly beings
which the Lord has created, not merely the angels. This includes the
seraphim, cherubim, and the living creatures.

While the fact that these "sons of God" came to "present themselves before the Lord" (Job 1:6) may limit this to angels who would

periodically report their activities, this is not necessarily the case. Basically, we just do not have enough information to know for certain.

3. THEY WERE CREATED BEFORE THE SEVENTH DAY

One thing we can be certain about is that the angels were created before the seventh day of creation. The Bible says the following about the six days of creation.

> Thus the heavens and the earth were finished, and all the host of them (Genesis 2:1 ESV).

The phrase "and all the host of them" probably refers to the angels as well as all the other heavenly beings which the Lord had made.

4. GOD CREATED ALL THINGS IN SIX DAYS

Another passage that is explicit about what God created is found in the Book of Exodus. It reads as follows.

> In six days the LORD made heaven, earth, and the sea, along with everything in them. He didn't work on the seventh day. That's why the LORD blessed the day he stopped his work and set this day apart as holy (Exodus 20:11 God's Word).

Everything was created in six days. This, of course, may include the angels. However, if the Bible is merely concerned about our present universe, the heaven and the earth, it is possible that angels were created at some time before our universe was formed.

5. THEY WERE PROBABLY ALL CREATED TOGETHER

From a statement that Paul made, it is sometimes assumed that all the angels were created together.

> Christ is the one through whom God created everything in heaven and earth. He made the things we can see and the

things we can't see— kings, kingdoms, rulers, and authorities. Everything has been created through him and for him (Colossians 1:16 NLT).

Although this may be true, it does not necessarily follow from this statement.

Therefore, from the available evidence contained in Scripture, we have no clear teaching as to when the angels were created.

SUMMARY TO QUESTION 7
WHEN WERE ANGELS CREATED?

The time of the creation of angels is something that the Bible does not specifically tell us. Angelic existence dates back before the creation of humans but just how far back no one knows.

They seem to have been in existence when the earth was created. In fact, Scripture may indicate that the angels sang and shouted at God's creation of the earth—possibly before any material thing was made. They were definitely created before humanity. Beyond this, there is not enough information to be more specific.

QUESTION 8

Were All The Angels
Created Good?

Yes. When God originally created the angels, they, along with every-thing else in the universe, were created good. The Bible says.

> Then God saw everything that He had made, and indeed it was very good. So the evening and the morning were the sixth day (Genesis 1:31 NKJV).

When God created the universe, everything that God had made was very good.

THIS MAY NOT BE SPEAKING OF THE ORIGINAL CREATION

This above statement, however, may not include the original creation of angels. Indeed, they may have been created before the Lord made the material universe. Yet, we assume that they were all created good in the beginning for a number of reasons.

GOD DOES NOT CREATE EVIL

First, God cannot make anything that is evil. Add to this, the devil and his angels are consistently spoken of in Scripture as rebelling against the Lord. For them to rebel it assumes they were created in a non-rebellious state. In other words, they were created as perfect beings. We go into great detail about this question in the next book in our series, "Evil Angels, Demons, and the Occult."

Here's what we do know when we examine the totality of Scripture.

1. THERE MAY HAVE BEEN A TIME OF PROBATION

Though all of the angels were originally created holy, not all of them remained in this state. It is possible that God allowed for a time of testing after their creation. Led by a particular created spirit-being, one of the cherubim, some of the angels rebelled against God. However, it does seem that most of them continued to follow the Lord. Whatever the case may be, the Bible makes a clear distinction between these two groups of angels, the good ones and the evil ones.

2. THERE ARE GOOD ANGELS WHO STAYED LOYAL TO GOD

The angels that did not rebel continue to follow the Lord until this day. They have constantly demonstrated their loyalty to God. They are known, among other descriptions, as the "elect" angels. When Paul wrote to Timothy he referred to them.

> I charge you, in the sight of God and Christ Jesus and the elect angels, to keep these instructions without partiality, and to do nothing out of favoritism (1 Timothy 5:21 NIV).

These good angels have remained loyal to God.

3. THERE ARE EVIL ANGELS WHO REBELLED

On the other hand, the Bible speaks of certain angels who rebelled against the Lord. Jude wrote the following about them.

> You also know that the angels who did not keep within their proper domain but abandoned their own place of residence, he has kept in eternal chains in utter darkness, locked up for the judgment of the great Day (Jude 6 NET).

Therefore, not all of the angels remained holy and committed to the Lord.

4. THE EVIL ANGELS ARE AWAITING THEIR PUNISHMENT

The evil angels now awaiting their punishment. The Bible says that the eternal fires of punishment were prepared for them. Jesus put it this way.

> Then he will say to those on his left, 'Depart from me, you who are cursed, into the eternal fire prepared for the devil and his angels' (Matthew 25:41 NIV).

There is punishment coming for these evil angels.

Consequently, Scripture teaches that all angels were created good but that some of them decided, on their own, to rebel against the Lord. This is why we have evil angels today.

In sum, we discover from Scripture that there are angels both good and bad.

SUMMARY TO QUESTION 8
WERE ALL THE ANGELS CREATED GOOD?

The Bible says that God initially created everything perfect. This includes the creation of angels. There was no imperfection in them whatsoever.

However, Scripture also indicates that some of the angels rebelled and chose to disobey the Lord. That rebellion separated the angels into two groups; the righteous and the unrighteous.

The righteous ones will remain in His service forever while the unrighteous angels, through their own choice, have been condemned to everlasting punishment. Their punishment is certain.

QUESTION 9

What Do Angels
Look Like?

Is there any indication in Scripture that angels are fair-skinned men who sit on clouds, wear long white robes, and have two large wings? Do we ever find them carrying harps?

Though this is the traditional way in which angels have been viewed, there is nothing in Scripture to suggest that this is how they look. From Scripture we learn a number of things about the appearance of angels.

1. THEY ARE SPIRIT BEINGS

Angels are spirit beings. There is no description given in the Bible of what they look like in their true essence. Although angels do not have a physical form like humans, they do seem to have some type of localized form—they occupy some space.

Whatever their normal form is like, it is a form adapted to the unseen spiritual realm. Though the Bible does not comment about their usual form, it does say that there are various types of bodies in heaven as well as upon the earth. Paul wrote.

> For not all flesh is the same, but there is one kind for humans, another for animals, another for birds, and another for fish. There are heavenly bodies and earthly bodies, but the glory of the heavenly is of one kind, and the glory of the earthly is of another (1 Corinthians 15:39-40 ESV).

The New Living Translation explains it this way.

> And just as there are different kinds of seeds and plants, so also there are different kinds of flesh—whether of humans, animals, birds, or fish. There are bodies in the heavens, and there are bodies on earth. The glory of the heavenly bodies is different from the beauty of the earthly bodies (1 Corinthians 15:39-40 NLT).

We cannot make any conclusions beyond this.

2. THEY USUALLY ARE NOT SEEN

In most cases, people do not see angels. In their ordinary activities they are not visible to the human eye. For example, the prophet Balaam could not see the angel standing in front of him in the road.

> When the donkey saw the Angel of the Lord standing on the path with a drawn sword in His hand, she turned off the path and went into the field. So Balaam hit her to return her to the path (Numbers 22:23 HCSB).

Elisha the prophet prayed that the eyes of his servant would be opened to see the angels around him.

> Then Elisha prayed, "Lord, please open his eyes and let him see." So the Lord opened the servant's eyes. He looked and saw that the mountain was covered with horses and chariots of fire all around Elisha (2 Kings 6:17 HCSB).

The "chariots of fire" is a term that refers to angels. Again, unless God allows them to be seen, they are invisible to us.

3. THEY ARE NOT ALWAYS RECOGNIZED AS ANGELS

That angels have no recognizable form can be observed as follows—many times they appeared to people without even being recognized as angels. They looked no different than ordinary men.

In the Book of Judges we read about one such episode. The Bible says the following.

> Then the woman went to her husband and told him, "A man of God came to me. He looked like an angel of God, very awesome. I didn't ask him where he came from, and he didn't tell me his name" . . . . When the angel of the LORD did not show himself again to Manoah and his wife, Manoah realized that it was the angel of the LORD (Judges 13:6,21 NIV).

The angel was described as a man with an awesome appearance.

Abraham had angelic visitors that looked human. The Book of Genesis says.

> The LORD appeared to Abraham by the oak trees belonging to Mamre as he was sitting at the entrance of his tent during the hottest part of the day. Abraham looked up, and suddenly he saw three men standing near him. When he saw them, he ran to meet them, and he bowed with his face touching the ground (Genesis 18:1,2 God's Word).

The angels were described initially as three men. In other words, they were not always recognized as angels.

4. THEY APPEAR AS MEN

Though angels are sexless creatures, when they appear in Scripture they are always described as looking like men; never women or children. For example, at the tomb of Jesus we are told that angels appeared. John writes.

> But Mary stood outside by the tomb weeping, and as she wept she stooped down and looked into the tomb. And she saw two angels in white sitting, one at the head and the other at the feet, where the body of Jesus had lain (John 20:11,12 NKJV).

John clearly states that two angels were at Jesus' tomb.

Yet Luke describes these angels as appearing in the form of men. We read.

> While they were perplexed about this, suddenly two men stood by them in dazzling clothes (Luke 24:4 HCSB).

Mark goes even further. He describes one of the angels at Jesus' tomb as a "young man."

> But when they looked up, they saw that the stone, which was very large, had been rolled away. As they entered the tomb, they saw a young man dressed in a white robe sitting on the right side, and they were alarmed (Mark 16: 4-5 NIV).

While angels appeared as men, the people soon recognized them as angels.

In addition, the two angels that are named in Scripture have names of men—Michael and Gabriel.

5. THEY ARE ABLE TO EAT

Angels, when they assume a human body, are able to eat. When three angels visited Abraham he prepared food for them.

> Then he took curds and milk and the calf that he had prepared, and set it before them; and he stood by them under the tree while they ate (Genesis 18:8 NRSV).

It has been noted that the psalmist wrote of the food of angels. He put it this way.

> Men ate angels' food; He sent them food to the full (Psalm 78:25 NKJV).

The New Living Translation says.

> They ate the food of angels! God gave them all they could hold. (Psalm 78:25 NLT).

Whatever the case may be, the phrase "food of angels" is not to be taken literally, since angels do not have bodies like ours which need food to exist.

6. THEY ARE CLOTHED

When angels appear, they are always clothed, sometimes in white or very bright clothing. In the gospel of Luke, we read the following.

> While they were perplexed about this, behold, two men suddenly stood near them in dazzling clothing (Luke 24:4 HCSB).

We find no darkness in them whatsoever as they are representing God—who Himself is light.

When Jesus ascended into heaven, two angels appeared wearing white clothes and having the appearance of men.

> While he was going and they were gazing up toward heaven, suddenly two men in white robes stood by them (Acts 1:10 NRSV).

At times, we find the angels wearing this bright clothing.

7. STEPHEN HAD THE FACE OF AN ANGEL

The martyr Stephen was said to have the face of an angel when he spoke to the religious rulers. We read about this in the Book of Acts.

> And all who sat in the council, looking steadfastly at him, saw his face as the face of an angel (Acts 6:15 NKJV).

The idea behind the phrase, "face of an angel," seems to be that his face was shining.

8. THEY REFLECT THE GLORY OF THE LORD

Sometimes the glory of the Lord shone through the angels. The Bible says the following.

Then an angel of the Lord stood before them, and the glory of the Lord shone around them, and they were terrified (Luke 2:9 NRSV).

God's glory is reflected in His creation, angels.

9. ANGELS SOMETIMES HAVE AN AWESOME APPEARANCE

Occasionally when angels appeared as men, they had an awesome appearance in either their size or in their clothing.

THE MOTHER OF SAMSON

The mother of Samson described her experience with an angel as follows.

A man of God came to me, and his appearance was like the appearance of the angel of God, very awesome. I did not ask him where he was from, and he did not tell me his name (Judges 13:6 ESV).

His appearance was certainly out of the ordinary.

DANIEL

When Daniel was visited by one particular angel, he described him in this manner.

On the twenty-fourth day of the first month, as I was standing on the bank of the great river (that is, the Tigris) I lifted up my eyes and looked, and behold, a man clothed in linen, with a belt of fine gold from Uphaz around his waist. His body was like beryl, his face like the appearance of lightning, his eyes like flaming torches, his arms and legs like the gleam of burnished bronze, and the sound of his words like the sound of a multitude (Daniel 10:4-6 ESV).

As to the exact identity of this angel there is much debate. Some see Him as God Himself taking on the form of an angel while others believe that this being was merely a high ranking angel. Since this personage is not identified for us any guess is only speculation.

THE ANGELS AT THE TOMB OF JESUS

On Easter Sunday, we find the following description of angels who were at the tomb of Jesus.

> While they were perplexed about this, behold, two men stood by them in dazzling apparel (Luke 24:4 ESV).

Though angels usually appear as normal looking men, there are times when they wear special clothing. Therefore, at times, angels did not appear like normal looking men.

10. THEY ARE NEVER APPEAR IN SUBHUMAN FORM

While the Bible records angels appearing at times in the form of humans, we never find them appearing in subhuman form. Indeed, they never appear to humans in the form of animals, birds, or fish.

11. THEY ARE IDENTIFIED WITH HUMANITY LIKE CHRIST

As Jesus Christ identified with humanity, by becoming a human being, angels, in a similar way as messengers of God, identified with humanity in outward form and language. They, as His messengers, come to humanity in a way that is identifiable to us.

12. THEY DO NOT HAVE WINGS

Medieval art made popular the idea that angels had wings. Though Daniel 9:21 and Revelation 14:6 refers to angels as flying, neither of these passages mentions wings. When angels have appeared to humans in the Bible, there is no indication that they had wings.

Though wings are never attributed to angels who have appeared to humanity, two other types of created spirit-beings—the cherubim and seraphim—have wings.

Apart from the cherubim guarding the Garden of Eden after the sin of Adam and Eve, there is no report in Scripture of their appearance to humans here upon the earth. The cherubim are seen in visions, or as representative figures in the Ark of the Covenant, and the temple.

In fact, we are not certain that Adam and Eve, or anyone else for that matter, actually saw the cherubim guarding Eden. Scripture does not specifically tell us.

Consequently, the idea that some heavenly beings do have wings does have some biblical validity. However, there is no indication in Scripture that angels have wings.

SUMMARY TO QUESTION 9
WHAT DO ANGELS LOOK LIKE?

Angels are spirit-beings who live in the unseen world. While their exact form is never described for us in Scripture, we know that they have no physical form like humans have.

When they have appeared to people in human-form, they always appeared as men, not women. They never appear as animals or in sub-human form. In certain instances they ate food in the presence of humans.

The concept that they appear as having white skin, with a halo over their heads, and playing a harp is not found in the Bible. None of these things are taught in Scripture.

The Bible teaches that two specific types of heavenly beings, the cherubim and seraphim, have wings.

However, there are no examples of angels ever appearing to humans with wings. This sums up what the Bible has to say on the subject.

Where Do Angels Live?

According to Scripture, earth is not the only inhabited place in the universe. There are angelic beings, as well as other heavenly beings which the Lord has created, who also reside in the universe.

From Scripture, we discover a number of things about where angels live and where they can and cannot go.

1. ANGELS LIVE IN HEAVEN

The Bible says that angels make their home in heaven. Jesus said.

> For when they rise from the dead, they neither marry nor are given in marriage, but are like angels in heaven (Mark 12:25 ESV).

Though they are said to live in the heavenly realm, there is not necessarily one certain place where they reside.

The Bible does speak of the evil angels leaving their proper dwelling or their "assigned place."

> He held angels for judgment on the great day. They were held in darkness, bound by eternal chains. These are the angels who didn't keep their position of authority but abandoned their assigned place (Jude 6 God's Word).

Some have thought that this refers to a specific place where angels reside. However, this is not clear from the text. What we can say for certain is that angels do live in the heavenly realm.

2. THEY HAVE ACCESS TO GOD

Not only do angels live in the heavenly realm, they also have access to God's presence. We read the following in the Book of Job.

> Now there was a day when the sons of God came to present themselves before the LORD, and Satan also came among them (Job 1:6 NKJV).

As we mentioned earlier, the "sons of God" referred to here may be angels. However, it is also possible this designation refers to some other type of spirit-being that the Lord created; such as the cherubim, seraphim, or the living creatures. We do not have enough information to be certain. Yet we do assume that these righteous angels do have access to God.

In addition, Scripture makes a distinction between the stellar heavens—the sun, moon, and stars—and the presence of God. His presence is above this stellar heavens. This is a place that no telescope can reach. The Bible says Christ entered into this realm after His death.

> Christ didn't go into a holy place made by human hands. He didn't go into a model of the real thing. Instead, he went into heaven to appear in God's presence on our behalf (Hebrews 9:24 God's Word).

Angels, as well as the other spirit-beings, have access to God in this special place where the Lord dwells in a unique way.

3. THEY CAN COME TO THE EARTH

While angels reside in heaven, and have access to God, the Bible says that they have the capacity to come to earth.

He had a dream in which he saw a stairway resting on the earth, with its top reaching to heaven, and the angels of God were ascending and descending on it (Genesis 28:12 NIV).

Scripture gives abundant testimony of angels leaving their home in heaven to minister here upon the earth.

For example, the Bible says an angel came down from heaven and rolled away the stone from Jesus' tomb.

And suddenly there was a great earthquake; for an angel of the Lord, descending from heaven, came and rolled back the stone and sat on it (Matthew 28:2 NRSV).

Angels have access to earth.

To sum up, while angels have a home in the heavenly realm they seemingly have access to anywhere in the universe.

SUMMARY TO QUESTION 10
WHERE DO ANGELS LIVE?

The Bible says that angels live in the unseen heavenly realm. Scripture teaches that they have access to God, whose presence dwells above the stellar heavens, the sun, the moon, and the stars.

Though angels have their residence in heaven, they are able to come to the earth. Therefore they are not restricted to any part of the universe. Consequently, they do the will of God wherever they are needed, whether on earth or in heaven.

Are Angels
Organized In Ranks?

Scripture teaches that God is a God of order. Paul told the church at Corinth that God wants everything done orderly.

> But everything should be done in a fitting and orderly way (1 Corinthians 14:40 NIV).

There is the need for things to be done orderly.

ANGELS ARE ORGANIZED

Therefore, it is not surprising that we find that Scripture testifying to various orders of angels. Paul wrote to the Colossians.

> Christ is the one through whom God created everything in heaven and earth. He made the things we can see and the things we can't see— kings, kingdoms, rulers, and authorities. Everything has been created through him and for him (Colossians 1:16 NLT).

The thrones, dominions, rulers, and powers speak of various orders of angels, as well as other heavenly beings, which the Lord has created. Each of these terms has a specific meaning that corresponds to earthly realities. Though there is probably some overlap between the terms, it does say, at the very least, that there are different ranks of angels as well as these other heavenly beings.

These various orders are well-organized. We read the following in the Old Testament.

> Then Micaiah said, "Therefore hear the word of the LORD: I saw the LORD sitting on His throne, and all the host of heaven standing by, on His right hand and on His left" (1 Kings 22:19 NKJV).

There are heavenly beings, some are on the right side of the Lord, the place of authority while others are on His left side.

THEY ARE LIKE AN ARMY

Their organization is like that of an army. The chronicler wrote.

> From day to day, men came to help David until he had an army as large as God's army (1 Chronicles 12:22 God's Word).

Angels operate like an army, well-organized and disciplined.

THEY HAVE AN ARCHANGEL

There is an archangel, or chief angel, according to Scripture. Paul wrote.

> For the Lord himself, with a cry of command, with the archangel's call and with the sound of God's trumpet, will descend from heaven, and the dead in Christ will rise first (1 Thessalonians 4:16 NRSV).

Scripture tells us that his name is Michael.

> But even Michael, one of the mightiest of the angels, did not dare accuse Satan of blasphemy, but simply said, "The Lord rebuke you." (This took place when Michael was arguing with Satan about Moses' body (Jude 9 NLT).

He is the only archangel named in Scripture, though there may be others.

Michael the archangel has his own army of angels. We read about this in the Book of Revelation.

And there was war in heaven: Michael and his angels fought against the dragon; and the dragon fought and his angels (Revelation 12:7 NRSV).

An army with a leader suggests organization.

THEY ARE ORGANIZED IN A NUMBER OF WAYS

According to the Bible, there are also angels that have authority over certain elements. They include fire, water, and the bottomless pit.

1. THERE IS AN ANGEL IN CHARGE OF THE FIRE

Scripture tells us of an angel who has authority over the fire. We read about this in the Book of Revelation.

Another angel came out of the temple in heaven, and he too had a sharp sickle. Still another angel, who had charge of the fire, came from the altar and called in a loud voice to him who had the sharp sickle, "Take your sharp sickle and gather the clusters of grapes from the earth's vine, because its grapes are ripe" (Revelation 14:17,18 NIV).

In some sense, this particular angel has authority over the fire.

2. THERE IS AN ANGEL IN CHARGE OF THE WATER

There is also an angel who has charge over the waters. We also read in the Book of Revelation.

The third angel poured out his bowl on the rivers and springs of water, and they became blood. Then I heard the angel in charge of the waters say: "You are just in these judgments, O Holy One, you who are and who were" (Revelation 16:4,5 NIV).

73

Again, in some unexplained sense, this particular angel has authority over the water.

3. THERE IS AN ANGEL OVER THE BOTTOMLESS PIT

There is also an angel who has authority over the bottomless pit, the abyss. We read the following in the Book of Revelation.

> Then the fifth angel blew his trumpet, and I saw a star that had fallen to earth from the sky, and he was given the key to the shaft of the bottomless pit. When he opened it, smoke poured out as though from a huge furnace, and the sunlight and air were darkened by the smoke (Revelation 9:1,2 NLT).

The Lord has put an angel in charge over the bottomless pit. Exactly what his duties are, we are not told.

In sum, from the different accounts we read in Scripture we discover that angels are highly organized, having specific duties to carry out.

SUMMARY TO QUESTION 11
ARE ANGELS ORGANIZED IN RANKS?

The God of the Bible is a God of order. Therefore, it is not surprising that the Bible says that angels are well-organized in ranks. While we are not told much about their classifications, we do know that there are various orders of angelic beings.

Among the orders of angels are those who have authority over the various elements. We are told from Scripture that certain angels have authority over fire, water, and the bottomless pit, the abyss.

This is a further testimony that angels are organized. The Bible also says that an archangel or "chief angel" exists. This also suggests organization. Beyond this, we can only conjecture.

QUESTION 12

What Is The
Character Of Angels?

The Bible tells us much about the nature or character of angels. From a study of Scripture, we find them to be personal, intelligent beings who obey the will of God.

1. THEY ARE OBEDIENT

Angels are obedient to God's commandments. They do not hesitate to obey the Lord when He commands them. The Bible says they do His bidding.

> Praise the LORD, you his angels, you mighty ones who do his bidding, who obey his word (Psalm 103:20 NIV).

The angels obey their Lord. When the Lord commands them to do something, they do it.

2. THEY ARE HOLY

The angels were originally created as holy beings to serve God. Isaiah records the angels as saying.

> And one called to another: Holy, holy, holy is the Lord of Hosts; His glory fills the whole earth (Isaiah 6:3 HCSB).

The phrase, "the LORD of hosts" means He is the LORD over all of angels, as well as the other heavenly beings which He created. He is holy, these beings also reflect His holiness.

3. ANGELS ARE REVERENT

The highest activity of angels is the worship of God. We read about this in Nehemiah who gave the following testimony.

> You alone are the LORD. You made the heavens, even the highest heavens, and all their starry host, the earth and all that is on it, the seas and all that is in them. You give life to everything, and the multitudes of heaven worship you (Nehemiah 9:6 NIV).

The multitudes of heaven worship the Lord, the creator and sustainer of all things. This, of course, would include the angels.

The writer to the Hebrews wrote about the angels worshipping the Son.

> And then, when he presented his honored Son to the world, God said, "Let all the angels of God worship him" (Hebrews 1:6 NLT).

Angels continually praise and glorify God, usually in His presence in heaven. On one occasion, at the birth of Jesus, the angels came to the earth.

> And suddenly there was with the angel a multitude of the heavenly host, praising God and saying, "Glory to God in the highest heaven, and on earth peace among those whom he favors!" (Luke 2:13,14 NRSV).

Angels have a reverence, or respect, for the Lord.

4. THEY CAN COMMUNICATE TO ANYONE

Language is no barrier for angels. Paul referred to the speaking ability of angels.

I may speak in the languages of humans and of angels. But if I don't have love, I am a loud gong or a clashing cymbal (1 Corinthians 13:1 God's Word).

Not only can angels speak, they can communicate to any people, in any language, on the face of the earth.

In fact, we find an angel preaching the everlasting gospel to the entire world before Christ returns.

Then I saw another angel flying high overhead, having the eternal gospel to announce to the inhabitants of the earth—to every nation, tribe, language, and people (Revelation 14:6 HCSB).

Every language was able to understand the message of this angel, there were no exceptions.

5. THEY ARE INTELLIGENT CREATURES

When the angels were created, they were made as intelligent spirits. They have been learning from the time they were created—having had the opportunity to observe God's dealings with humanity.

In addition, their intelligence has not been corrupted by sin, as is the case with humanity. Therefore their wisdom is beyond that of humans. Scripture acknowledges their ability. The wise woman of Tekoa said the following to King David.

Your servant Joab did this to change the present situation. My lord has wisdom like that of an angel of God—he knows everything that happens in the land (2 Samuel 14:20 NIV).

77

Interestingly, we have the phrase "the wisdom like that of an angel of God." Obviously, angels are assumed to have wisdom far above that which we humans possess.

6. THEY HAVE LIMITED KNOWLEDGE

Though angels have superior intelligence to humans, their knowledge is limited. God cannot add to His knowledge because He knows everything. The same thing cannot be said of angels. They can continue to learn.

In fact, the Bible says there are certain things which they do not know. For example, they do not know the time of Jesus' return to the earth.

> Now concerning that day and hour no one knows—neither the angels in heaven, nor the Son—except the Father only (Matthew 24:36 HCSB).

Furthermore, Scripture tells us there are some things that they have desired to know.

> It was revealed to them that they were serving not themselves but you, in regard to the things that have now been announced to you through those who brought you good news by the Holy Spirit sent from heaven—things into which angels long to look! (1 Peter 1:12 NRSV).

In this instance, it is prophetic matters the angels are interested in, things having to do with the future.

We also find this in the Book of Daniel where two angels are discussing the meaning of certain things that the prophet Daniel was told. The Bible records what happened as follows.

> But you, Daniel, keep these words secret and seal the book until the time of the end. Many will roam about, and knowledge will increase. Then I, Daniel, looked, and two others

were standing there, one on this bank of the river and one on the other. One of them said to the man dressed in linen, who was above the waters of the river, "How long until the end of these extraordinary things" (Daniel 12:4-6 HCSB).

Interestingly, these angelic figures were interested in future events, therefore, they asked how long would it be until these things came to pass.

However, we find that only God knows what is in the human heart. The Bible records the following request of King Solomon.

> May You hear in heaven, Your dwelling place, and may You forgive, act, and repay the man, according to all his ways, since You know his heart, for You alone know every human heart (1 Kings 8:39 HCSB).

As intelligent as angels may be, they are still limited in what they know.

7. ANGELS KNOW RIGHT FROM WRONG

Angels do know the difference between right and wrong, good from evil. We read about this in Second Samuel. It says.

> Yes, the king will give us peace of mind again. I know that you are like an angel of God and can discern good from evil. May the LORD your God be with you (2 Samuel 14:17 NLT).

The fact that angels could discern good from evil was a proverbial expression in the nation Israel.

8. THEY ARE MIGHTY IN POWER BUT DEPENDENT UPON GOD

Angels are greater than humans in power. Peter wrote the following.

> Whereas angels, who are greater in power and might, do not bring a reviling accusation against them before the Lord (2 Peter 2:11 NKJV).

The Psalmist wrote.

> Bless the LORD, O you his angels, you mighty ones who do his bidding, obedient to his spoken word (Psalm 103:20 NRSV).

They are called Christ's mighty angels.

> And God will provide rest for you who are being persecuted and also for us when the Lord Jesus appears from heaven. He will come with his mighty angels (2 Thessalonians 1:7 NLT).

Angels are able to do things that humans cannot do. However their power is dependent upon God. They are mighty beings, but angels are not the Almighty. Their power is within fixed limits. Any power that angels may have is derived from God, and from Him alone.

Indeed, they are neither all-powerful, all-knowing, or everywhere present, as is God. If there were another being in the universe that was all-powerful, then God would not be the only God.

EXAMPLES OF THE LIMITED POWER OF ANGELS

The fact that angels are not all-powerful can be seen in the episode of Michael, the archangel, and Satan. The Bible records what happened as follows.

> But even Michael, one of the mightiest of the angels, did not dare accuse Satan of blasphemy, but simply said, "The Lord rebuke you." (This took place when Michael was arguing with Satan about Moses' body" (Jude 9 NLT).

Michael the archangel, the highest ranked of all the angels, would not rebuke the devil by himself. While angels are indeed superhuman in their strength, they themselves do not bring slanderous accusations against the devil. This is one example of how angels, while powerful, have limited power.

Unlike God, angels can be in only one place at a time. The Bible says the following about the angel Gabriel.

> In the sixth month of Elizabeth's pregnancy, God sent the angel Gabriel to Nazareth, a village in Galilee (Luke 1:26 NLT).

Since the Bible speaks of angels traveling from place to place this indicates they cannot be everywhere at once.

Daniel records this testimony of an angel.

> Then he continued, "Do not be afraid, Daniel. Since the first day that you set your mind to gain understanding and to humble yourself before your God, your words were heard, and I have come in response to them. But the prince of the Persian kingdom resisted me twenty-one days. Then Michael, one of the chief princes, came to help me, because I was detained there with the king of Persia. Now I have come to explain to you what will happen to your people in the future, for the vision concerns a time yet to come" (Daniel 10:12-14 NIV).

This passage shows the limitation of the power of angels, as well as the fact that they are not everywhere present.

9. THEY ARE HUMBLE

Though mighty, angels are also humble. They do not seek their own glory but rather the glory of God. They go about their ministry unnoticed by humanity.

10. GOOD ANGELS ARE SINLESS

The angels that did not rebel against Him are without sin. While this is never directly stated, it is inferred from the various names given to them. They are called both "holy angels" (Mark 8:38) and "elect angels" (1 Timothy 5:21).

In sum, we can learn many things about the character of angels from a study of Scripture. In fact, their unquestioned obedience to the Lord is an illustration of what each of us need to imitate.

SUMMARY TO QUESTION 12
WHAT IS THE CHARACTER OF ANGELS?

Some of the characteristics, or attributes, of angels are listed for us in Scripture. The Bible says they are obedient, holy, and reverent.

They are able to communicate to anyone. They are intelligent creatures but their knowledge is limited. They do know right from wrong.

Although they are mighty, they remain humble. In addition, the angels that did not rebel against God are without sin.

There is much for us to learn from them. Though powerful, they are humble. Though intelligent, they have devoted their intelligence to the service of the Lord. This is an example which we should follow.

QUESTION 13

What Are Some Of The Names Given To Angels?

Apart from the familiar title "angel," these heavenly beings are known by a variety of different names in the Bible. As we search the Scripture we find them designated as follows.

1. ANGELS

This, of course, is their most popular name. Often when we find these spirit-beings addressed as angels, there are qualifying words that further describe them. These include the following.

Jesus called them "holy angels."

> For whoever is ashamed of Me and My words, of him the Son of Man will be ashamed when He comes in His own glory, and in His Father's, and of the holy angels (Luke 9:26 NRSV).

Christ also called them the "angels of God."

> And I tell you, everyone who acknowledges me before men, the Son of Man also will acknowledge before the angels of God, but the one who denies me before men will be denied before the angels of God (Luke 12:8 ESV).

On one occasion, the Lord called them "His angels."

For the Son of Man is to come with his angels in the glory of his Father, and then he will repay everyone for what has been done (Matthew 16:27 NRSV).

These beings are also known as the "angels in heaven."

For when the dead rise, they won't be married. They will be like the angels in heaven (Matthew 22:30 NLT).

The Bible also calls them "mighty angels."

And God will provide rest for you who are being persecuted and also for us when the Lord Jesus appears from heaven. He will come with his mighty angels (2 Thessalonians 1:7 NLT).

These angels are mighty.

Therefore, with the term "angel," we find a number of qualifiers giving us further insight into their character.

2. THE HOST OF HEAVEN (HEAVENLY HOST)

Scripture designates angels as the "host of heaven" or the "heavenly host." We read the following in Luke.

And suddenly there was with the angel a multitude of the heavenly host praising God and saying (Luke 2:13 ESV).

This term refers to the armies of angels. The angels, as the "host of heaven," are represented as standing on both the right and left side of God.

Then Micaiah said, "Therefore hear the word of the LORD: I saw the LORD sitting on His throne, and all the host of heaven standing by, on His right hand and on His left" (1 Kings 22:19 NKJV).

The Bible continually refers to God as the "God of hosts" or the "LORD of hosts." The word "hosts" also refers to the stars in the sky in certain contexts.

3. SPIRITS

Angels are also known as spirits. The writer to the Hebrews put it this way.

> Are not all angels spirits in the divine service, sent to serve for the sake of those who are to inherit salvation? (Hebrews 1:14 NRSV).

This speaks of their nature; they are spirit-beings. Indeed, angels are spirits; supernatural heavenly beings. However, as we have noted, God has created other spirit-beings that are distinct from the angels. These beings are not heavenly messengers as are the angels.

4. SONS OF GOD

In the Book of Job, we find the phrase the "sons of God." It says.

> Now there was a day when the sons of God came to present themselves before the LORD, and Satan also came among them (Job 1:6 NKJV).

A "son of God" is one who is brought into existence by God. They are sons of God in the sense that they are His creation. This is seemingly how angels are described by the Lord in this context. We say "seemingly" because the phrase may be describing other created beings apart from the angels such as the cherubim, seraphim, and the living creatures.

Interestingly, instead of the phrase, "sons of God," the New International Version translates this as follows.

> One day the angels came to present themselves before the LORD, and Satan also came with them (Job 1:6 NIV).

A number of other English translations also render the Hebrew phrase "sons of God" as angels in this context. However, this goes further than what the text states. While these heavenly personages may indeed be angels it could also be speaking of other spirit-beings which the Lord created.

5. SONS OF THE MIGHTY, MIGHTY ONES

In some translations, angels are called "sons of the mighty" or the "mighty ones." The psalmist wrote the following.

> For who in the heavens can be compared to the Lord? Who among the sons of the mighty can be likened to the Lord (Psalm 89:6 NKJV).

They are also called mighty ones.

> Give unto the Lord, O you mighty ones, Give unto the Lord glory and strength (Psalm 29:1 NKJV).

Other translations are less specific in this reference. Instead of using the term "sons of the mighty," or mighty ones, they say "heavenly beings."

> Give to the Lord, you heavenly beings. Give to the Lord glory and power (Psalm 29:1 God's Word).

In addition, still other translations used the term "angels" here.

> All of you angels in heaven, honor the glory and power of the LORD (Psalms 29:1 CEV).

Angels, who have their origin in heaven, are given their strength by the Lord. That is why they can be called mighty.

There is something else we should consider. Since this passage seemingly refers to *all* of the host of heaven, it would include all of the other spirit-beings, apart from the angels, which the Lord has created.

6. HOLY ONES, SAINTS

Angels are also called "holy ones" by the psalmist.

> The heavens praise your wonders, O LORD, your faithfulness too, in the assembly of the holy ones. For who in the skies above can compare with the LORD? Who is like the LORD among the heavenly beings? In the council of the holy ones God is greatly feared; he is more awesome than all who surround him (Psalm 89:5-7 NIV).

This emphasizes that angels are separated unto the Lord. This is the idea behind being "holy."

The "council of the holy ones" may or may not refer specifically to angels. As we have repeatedly mentioned, God has created other heavenly beings that have a different function than the angels.

We find the same words in the New Testament of the angels.

> Now Enoch, the seventh in descent beginning with Adam, even prophesied of them, saying, "Look! The Lord is coming with thousands and thousands of his holy ones, to execute judgment on all, and to convict every person of all their thoroughly ungodly deeds that they have committed, and of all the harsh words that ungodly sinners have spoken against him" (Jude 14-15 NET).

Jude quoted a prophecy made by Enoch which spoke of the return of Jesus Christ to the earth accompanied by thousands upon thousands of His holy ones, angels.

Some translations call them "saints."

> Now Enoch, the seventh from Adam, prophesied about these men also, saying, "Behold, the Lord comes with ten thousands of His saints" (Jude 14 NKJV).

However, using the term "saints" is confusing because this is a word that is consistently used of believers. Angels are in view in this passage.

7. THE WATCHERS (SENTINELS)

In the Book of Daniel, angels are called "watchers" by the pagan King Nebuchadnezzar. He explained what he saw in this manner.

> I saw in the visions of my head as I lay in bed, and behold, a watcher, a holy one, came down from heaven. He proclaimed aloud and said thus: 'Chop down the tree and lop off its branches, strip off its leaves and scatter its fruit. Let the beasts flee from under it and the birds from its branches ... The sentence is by the decree of the watchers, the decision by the word of the holy ones' (Daniel 4:13,14,17 ESV).

These beings are "watching;" they are looking out for the things of God.

Some translations use the word "sentinels" in describing them.

> While I was watching in my mind's visions on my bed, a holy sentinel came down from heaven (Daniel 4:13 NET).

The word literally means "one who is awake." The idea is that these angels are watching out for the things of God.

8. FLAMES OF FIRE

They are called "flames of fire." We read of this in the Book of Hebrews. It says.

> Who makes His angels spirits, His ministers a flame of fire (Psalm 104:4 NKJV).

Some translations think this refers to the wind, and not to angels. For example, the Contemporary English Version says.

The winds are your messengers, and flames of fire are your servants (Psalm 104:4 CEV).

If this is the case, then this would not be a reference to angels.

9. PRINCE, CHIEF PRINCES

Angels are called "princes," with one specific angel, Michael, called a "chief prince."

We read of this in the Book of Daniel.

But I will tell you what is inscribed in the book of truth: there is none who contends by my side against these except Michael, your prince (Daniel 10:21 ESV).

Earlier in this passage, Michael was called a "chief prince."

But the prince of the Persian kingdom resisted me twenty-one days. Then Michael, one of the chief princes, came to help me, because I was detained there with the king of Persia (Daniel 10:13 NIV).

Michael is one of the chief princes. Therefore, there has to be others. It seems that they rule in some unexplained way in the unseen world.

10. THRONES

In some translations, angels are called thrones.

For everything was created by Him, in heaven and on earth, the visible and the invisible, whether thrones or dominions or rulers or authorities—all things have been created through Him and for Him. (Colossians 1:16 HCSB).

This title is symbolic of leadership. Other translations emphasize the leadership of angels.

Christ is the one through whom God created everything in heaven and earth. He made the things we can see and the things we can't see— kings, kingdoms, rulers, and authorities. Everything has been created through him and for him (Colossians 1:16 NLT).

They have the capability of leading.

11. DOMINIONS

This speaks of their sphere of influence. We read in the same verse in Colossians. It says.

For everything was created by Him, in heaven and on earth, the visible and the invisible, whether thrones or dominions or rulers or authorities—all things have been created through Him and for Him. (Colossians 1:16 HCSB).

Angels have influence in the unseen realm.

12. POWERS

This is another term for rulers. Again, we cite the statement of Paul to the Colossians.

Christ is the one through whom God created everything in heaven and earth. He made the things we can see and the things we can't see—kings, kingdoms, rulers, and authorities. Everything has been created through him and for him (Colossians 1:16 NLT).

Powers is another way of saying "rulers."

13. THE ELECT

The good angels are given the title of "elect." Paul wrote the following to Timothy.

I charge you before God and the Lord Jesus Christ and the elect angels that you observe these things without prejudice, doing nothing with partiality (1 Timothy 5:21 NKJV).

The elect are the ones chosen by the Lord to do His bidding.

14. CHARIOTS OF FIRE

Angels are also called "chariots of fire." We read of this description in Second Kings.

Then Elisha prayed, "Lord, please open his eyes and let him see." So the Lord opened the servant's eyes. He looked and saw that the mountain was covered with horses and chariots of fire all around Elisha (2 Kings 6:17 HCSB).

This title speaks of an angelic army.

15. THE HEAVENLY COUNCIL (ASSEMBLY)

Angels are seemingly spoken of as being a council, or an assembly, of holy ones. We read the following in the Book of Psalms.

The heavens praise your wonders, O LORD, your faithfulness too, in the assembly of the holy ones. For who in the skies above can compare with the LORD? Who is like the LORD among the heavenly beings? In the council of the holy ones God is greatly feared; he is more awesome than all who surround him (Psalm 89:5-7 NIV).

This description of the "council of the holy ones" may or may not include angels. Remember there are other heavenly beings that the Lord has created, the cherubim, seraphim, and the living creatures. They may be the ones in view here. Since angels, are God's messengers, they may not have been included in this heavenly council.

16. HEAVENLY BEINGS

They are also called heavenly beings. The psalmist wrote.

> Ascribe to the Lord, O heavenly beings, ascribe to the Lord glory and strength (Psalm 29:1 ESV).

This description points out their heavenly origin. While this can, of course, refer to angels, it may be speaking of all the heavenly beings which the Lord has created.

17. MORNING STARS

The title "morning stars" is found in the Book of Job.

> When the morning stars sang together, and all the sons of God shouted for joy? (Job 38:7 NKJV).

This could be a title of angels, a title of other heavenly beings apart from the angels, or it could be symbolically referring to God's creation.

18. ANGEL OF LIGHT

Interestingly, one of the designations for the righteous angels is the term "angel of light." However, it is only used in describing the deception of the devil. We read the following.

> For such people are false apostles, deceitful workers, masquerading as apostles of Christ. And no wonder, for Satan himself masquerades as an angel of light. It is not surprising, then, if his servants also masquerade as servants of righteousness. Their end will be what their actions deserve (2 Corinthians 11:13-15 NIV).

To sum up, these various titles of angels, which we find in Scripture, give us insight into their unique character. They are helpful in determining much about them.

SUMMARY TO QUESTION 13
WHAT ARE SOME OF THE NAMES GIVEN TO ANGELS?

The Bible attributes a number of names and titles to angels. They include angels, host of heaven, spirits, sons of God, sons of the Mighty, holy ones, the watchers, flames of fire, rulers, thrones, dominions, powers, the elect, chariots of fire, the council, heavenly beings and morning stars.

Each of these titles helps us to better understand their attributes. It is interesting to note just how many different descriptions the Bible gives of angels—obviously they have been very busy in carrying out God's plan of the ages.

What Do Angels And Humans Have In Common?

While angels and humans are different types of beings, they do have a number of things in common. The evidence is as follows.

1. BOTH ANGELS AND HUMANS WERE CREATED

First, both angels and humans have been created by God. The creation of the first human, Adam, is listed in the Book of Genesis. It reads as follows.

> Then the Lord God formed the man of dust from the ground and breathed into his nostrils the breath of life, and the man became a living creature (Genesis 2:7 ESV).

The angels were also created by God. However, they are spirit-beings; a different order of beings than are humans.

2. ANGELS AND HUMANS WERE CREATED BY JESUS CHRIST

Not only are both angels and humans created beings, it is Jesus Christ who created the angels as well as creating humanity.

The Gospel of John says that the Word, or Jesus Christ, created all things.

> In the beginning the Word already existed. The Word was with God, and the Word was God. He was already with God

in the beginning. Everything came into existence through him. Not one thing that exists was made without him (John 1:1-3 God's Word).

All things were created by Jesus, including humans and angels. Paul wrote the Colossians.

Christ is the visible image of the invisible God. He existed before God made anything at all and is supreme over all creation. Christ is the one through whom God created everything in heaven and earth. He made the things we can see and the things we can't see— kings, kingdoms, rulers, and authorities. Everything has been created through him and for him (Colossians 1:15,16 NLT).

The testimony of God's Word is that Jesus created everything.

3. ANGELS AND HUMANS ARE DEPENDENT CREATURES

Because angels and humans have been created by God, and have not existed eternally, both are dependent creatures. This means that they need something outside of themselves to exist. Unlike God who has life in Himself, angels and humans are not self-sustaining.

4. BOTH ANGELS AND HUMANS WERE CREATED PERFECT

Both angels and humans were created perfect in the beginning. The Bible has the following to say about God's finished creation.

Then God saw everything that He had made, and indeed it was very good. So the evening and the morning were the sixth day (Genesis 1:31 NKJV).

Everything that God created was very good. The angels served the Lord God in His heavenly presence while perfect humanity was placed upon the earth.

5. SIN ENTERED THE ANGELIC AND HUMAN REALM

Sin has entered both the angelic and human realms. The entrance of sin as far as the human race is concerned is recorded in the third chapter of Genesis. We are not certain when the angelic rebellion occurred but we do know that it had happened before the time the serpent tempted Eve.

6. THE SAME PERSONAGE WAS RESPONSIBLE FOR SIN ENTERING BOTH REALMS

The Bible says that the same personage, Satan or the devil, was the one responsible for bringing sin into the earthly and the heavenly realm. He was the one behind the serpent in the Garden of Eden. He is also the one who led the angelic rebellion. Jesus said he was the father of all lies.

> For you are the children of your father the Devil, and you love to do the evil things he does. He was a murderer from the beginning and has always hated the truth. There is no truth in him. When he lies, it is consistent with his character; for he is a liar and the father of lies (John 8:44 NLT).

Angelic and human sin came about from the instigation of this one personage.

7. BELIEVERS AND RIGHTEOUS ANGELS ARE FELLOW SERVANTS OF THE LORD

According to the angel that the Apostle John attempted to worship, the righteous angels and the believing humans are both fellow-servants of the Lord. We read the following.

> I, John, am the one who heard and saw these things. And when I heard and saw them, I fell down to worship at the feet of the angel who showed them to me, but he said to me, "You must not do that! I am a fellow servant with you and your brothers the prophets, and with those who keep the words of this book. Worship God" (Revelation 22:8 ESV).

The words of the angel to John are highly instructive. Not only are angels not to be worshipped by humans, the righteous angels and the redeemed humans are fellow servants of the Lord.

In other words, angels and humans are placed on the same level, we are all here to serve the Lord. Therefore, as this angel testified, we are never to exalt angels, or see them as beings to whom we are to bow down, or to serve them. Instead, we are all servants together.

8. UNRIGHTEOUS ANGELS AND UNBELIEVING HUMANS WILL BE PUNISHED BY GOD

Judgment, and then punishment, is coming to both unrighteous humans and evil angels. Since there was sin in both realms, and seeing that God cannot tolerate sin, there must be punishment.

9. ANGELS AND HUMANS WILL EXIST ETERNALLY

Though there has been sin among angels and humans neither will be annihilated. God has made angels and humans to have eternal or everlasting existence. In other words, there will never come a time when they cease to exist.

10. CERTAIN ANGELS AND CERTAIN HUMANS WILL BE WITH GOD FOR ALL ETERNITY

Humans, who have believed in the Lord, as well as the righteous angels, will spend eternity in His presence. This is the wonderful promise of Scripture.

11. SOME ANGELS AND SOME HUMANS WILL BE SEPARATED FROM GOD

While the initial punishment of angels has taken place in the distant past there will be a final judgment, and then punishment, for both unbelieving humanity as well as the sinning angels in the future. Indeed, Jesus said the wicked will be sent to the same "lake of fire" as the devil and his angels.

Then he will say to those on his left, 'Depart from me, you who are cursed, into the eternal fire prepared for the devil and his angels' (Matthew 25:41 NIV).

The sinning angels, as well as those humans who have rejected Christ, will be eternally punished for their sin. This does not, however, mean that they will be destroyed, or annihilated (for more information on this subject see our book on "Hell").

This sums up the many things which we humans have in common with angels.

SUMMARY TO QUESTION 14
WHAT DO ANGELS AND HUMANS HAVE IN COMMON?

From the Bible, we discover that there are a number of things that angels, invisible spirit beings, have in common with humans.

To begin with, angels and humans are created beings, neither have existed eternally. Also, we find that Jesus Christ created both angels and humans. Scripture emphasizes that He is the Creator of all things, both visible and invisible.

Because angels and humans are created beings, they are dependent creatures. In other words, they need something apart from themselves to exist. Consequently, each is dependent upon God for their continued existence.

There is also the fact that the righteous angels and the believing humans are fellow servants together. In fact, when John attempted to worship an angel he was rebuked. The angel made it clear that humans and angels, while different orders of beings, are on the same level as fellow servants of the Lord. Therefore, angels should never be exalted or worshipped.

Angels and humans were initially created perfect. However, sin entered into both the angelic and human realm. Consequently, the visible as well as the invisible realm has been marred by sin.

The Bible says that the same personage was responsible for bringing sin into both realms. He is a sinful created spirit-being known as Satan or the devil.

Because there has been sin in angelic and human realms, there will be a day of judgment for both angels and humans. This judgment will lead to everlasting punishment for the wicked.

While there is punishment for both evil angels and wicked humanity, neither will be annihilated. God has created angels and humans to exist forever.

On the other hand, those humans who have believed in the Lord will spend eternity with Him along with the angels who did not sin.

Consequently, as we examine what the Bible has to say about angels and humans, we find that we do have a number of things in common.

What Are The Differences Between Angels And Humans?

The Bible says that angels have certain things in common with humans. For example, both angels and humans were created by God. In addition, angels are humans were created by Jesus Christ.

In addition, angels and humans are dependent creatures, they need something apart from themselves to exist.

Sin affected both the human and the angelic realm. Therefore, both the wicked angels and the unbelieving humans will be judged and then punished by God for their wickedness.

These are some of the things which we have in common.

However, while angels and humans have things in common, there are also a number of differences between them. They are as follows.

1. HUMANS ARE CREATED IN GOD'S IMAGE, ANGELS ARE NOT

While both angels and human beings have been created by God, only humans, however, were created in the image of God. We read about the special creation of humanity in the Book of Genesis. The Bible puts it this way.

> Then God said, "Let us make people in our image, to be like ourselves. They will be masters over all life—the fish in the

sea, the birds in the sky, and all the livestock, wild animals, and small animals." So God created people in his own image; God patterned them after himself; male and female he created them (Genesis 1:26,27 NLT).

Only humans have been made in God's image. This fact makes us distinct from all creatures here upon earth as well as the angels in the heavenly realm.

2. THE ENTRANCE OF SIN TOUCHED ALL HUMANS BUT ONLY SOME OF THE ANGELS

Though humanity and angels were created perfect, sin touched both the human and angelic population. After Adam and Eve sinned, all the humans that were born afterward, with the exception of the Lord Jesus, were born with a sin nature. The Bible says.

When Adam had lived 130 years, he had a son in his own likeness, in his own image; and he named him Seth (Genesis 5:3 NIV).

The likeness of Adam was a sinful likeness. All humans who are born inherit that sin nature. The Bible says.

For all have sinned and fall short of the glory of God (Romans 3:23 NKJV).

Some angels also sinned. However many did not. Those that did not sin have remained loyal to God ever since.

3. HUMANS CAN BEAR CHILDREN, ANGELS CANNOT

Unlike humans, angels cannot bear children. These spirit-beings cannot, therefore, have any type of family relationships. Jesus said.

For in the resurrection they neither marry nor are given in marriage, but are like angels in heaven (Matthew 22:30 NRSV).

Only humans can marry, only humans can have children, and therefore only humans can have a family relationship.

4. HUMANS CAN BE FORGIVEN, ANGELS CANNOT

Though all humans and some angels sinned, forgiveness is only offered to sinful humans. Paul wrote the following to the Corinthians.

> For God made Christ, who never sinned, to be the offering for our sin, so that we could be made right with God through Christ (2 Corinthians 5:21 NLT).

The angels who sinned are awaiting the Day of Judgment. Jesus spoke of this day when they will be judged and then punished.

> Then the king will say to those on his left, 'Get away from me! God has cursed you! Go into everlasting fire that was prepared for the devil and his angels!' (Matthew 25:41 God's Word).

Angels have already made their choice. Therefore, no forgiveness has been offered to them.

5. HUMANS SHARE CHRIST'S EXALTED POSITION, ANGELS DO NOT

Believers are a new creation in Christ. Consequently we share His exalted position. Paul wrote to the Ephesians.

> [Christ] raised us up with him and seated us with him in the heavenly places in Christ Jesus (Ephesians 2:6 NRSV).

The New Living Translation puts it this way.

> For he raised us from the dead along with Christ, and we are seated with him in the heavenly realms—all because we are one with Christ Jesus (Ephesians 2:6 NLT).

Only humans can be raised in heavenly places in Christ. It is not possible for this to happen with angels.

6. HUMANS WILL CONFORM TO THE IMAGE OF JESUS CHRIST, ANGELS DO NOT

The final state of redeemed humans is far above angels—believers will be conformed to the image of Christ.

> Because those whom he foreknew he also predestined to be conformed to the image of his Son, that his Son would be the firstborn among many brothers and sisters (Romans 8:29 NET).

John also tells us that someday we will be like Jesus.

> Dear friends, we are God's children now, and what we will be has not yet been revealed. We know that when He appears, we will be like Him because we will see Him as He is (1 John 3:2 HCSB).

Believers will eventually be conformed to the image of Jesus Christ, we will be like Him! This is the wonderful future God has planned for us!

7. HUMANS WILL SOMEDAY JUDGE ANGELS, ANGELS WILL NOT JUDGE HUMANS

The humans who have believed in Jesus will eventually judge angels. Paul wrote the following to the Corinthians.

> Don't you realize that we Christians will judge angels? So you should surely be able to resolve ordinary disagreements here on earth (1 Corinthians 6:3 NLT).

We will judge them, they will not judge us.

Consequently, when we look at the totality of Scripture, we find that there are a number of differences between angels and humans.

SUMMARY TO QUESTION 15
WHAT ARE THE DIFFERENCES BETWEEN ANGELS AND HUMANS?

While there are some things that angels and humans have in common, there are many things that separate these two orders of created beings. They include the following.

Humans have been made in the image of God, this is not true of angels. In fact, humans are the only creation of God, on earth or in heaven, that bears the divine image.

Only humans are able to bear children and have family relationships, angels cannot. In fact, angels cannot marry, they are sexless creatures. Therefore, the angelic realm, once created could not increase neither could it decrease.

Though sin has entered into both the angelic and human sphere, only the sins of humans can be forgiven. Jesus Christ came to die for the sins of humanity, not the sins of angels. Those humans who have trusted Christ as their Savior will eventually judge angels.

Because of these things, the humans who have believed in Jesus will have a superior position to the angels in the ages to come, though now we are a lower order of being than they are.

This sums up some of the difference between us and the angels. As we have seen, we have things in common with them, as well as having a number of differences.

What Are The Differences Between Jesus And The Angels?

The Bible contrasts the character of angels and that of the Lord Jesus. From Scripture, we can note the following comparisons.

1. JESUS HAS A MORE EXCELLENT NAME

Jesus has a more excellent name than the angels. The writer to the Hebrews put it this way.

> So He became higher in rank than the angels, just as the name He inherited is superior to theirs (Hebrews 1:4 HCSB).

There is a clear distinction between Jesus and the angels. The word "name" in this context has to do with character.

For example, the angels named in Scripture are Michael "who is like God?" and Gabriel "God is my strength." Yet Jesus has a more excellent name than them in the sense that He is the Lord God Himself.

2. JESUS CHRIST IS SUPERIOR TO ANGELS IN EVERY RESPECT

In a long passage (Hebrews 1:5-2:9) the writer emphasizes Christ as superior to the angels in every respect. For a short time, when He became a human, God the Son was made a little lower than the angels. However, He is, in every way, superior to them.

3. ANGELS WORSHIP HIM

Christ is superior to the angels in the fact that they worship Him. We read about this in the Book of Hebrews.

> And again, when he brings the firstborn into the world, he says, "Let all God's angels worship him" (Hebrews 1:6 NRSV).

Angels are commanded to worship the God the Son. On the other hand, the Bible forbids any worship of angels.

4. HE IS THE CREATOR WHILE THEY ARE THE CREATED

We also see the contrast between the Creator and the created. In fact, Scripture teaches that Jesus was the Creator of the angels.

> Christ is the one through whom God created everything in heaven and earth. He made the things we can see and the things we can't see—kings, kingdoms, rulers, and authorities. Everything has been created through him and for him (Colossians 1:16 NLT).

Angels were created above humanity, but they are below Christ—the Creator of all things.

These are some of the differences between Jesus the Creator, and the angels, a created order. Consequently we should never equate Jesus with the angels in any way.

SUMMARY TO QUESTION 16
WHAT ARE THE DIFFERENCES BETWEEN JESUS AND THE ANGELS?

There are a number of differences between Jesus Christ and the angelic host. We can list them as follows.

For one thing, the Bible clearly says that Jesus has a more excellent name than the angels. He is certainly above the angels, superior in every respect.

The reason for this is simple. He is distinct from the angels in the fact that He created them. As the Creator of all things, Jesus is a different category of being. He is God, the Creator, while angels are the created, they have no eternal existence in the past while He has existed forever as God the Son.

Therefore we have the clear distinction between the Creator and the created. Consequently, this is why Jesus is said to have a more excellent name, or identity, than the angels. Indeed, there is really no comparison between Him and them.

What Have Angels Done According To The Old Testament?

Angels have figured prominently in many episodes that the Old Testament records. We will consider some of the more important examples.

1. THEY WERE PRESENT AT CREATION

When God created the world, it seems angels witnessed it. We read the questions that the Lord asked Job.

> Where were you when I laid the foundation of the earth? Tell me, if you possess understanding! Who set its measurements-if you know- or who stretched a measuring line across it? On what were its bases set, or who laid its cornerstone-when the morning stars a sang in chorus, and all the sons of God shouted for joy (Job 38:4-7 NET).

The angels, as well as the other heavenly beings which the Lord created, rejoiced at God's creative work.

2. AN ANGEL BROUGHT GOOD NEWS TO HAGAR

Although angels were seemingly present at creation, there is no mention of their ministry until the days of Abraham. After Hagar had conceived Abraham's child, Sarah, Abraham's wife, sent her out. The angel of the LORD found Hagar in the desert.

> The angel of the LORD found Hagar near a spring in the desert; it was the spring that is beside the road to Shur (Genesis 16:7 NIV).

Later, when Abraham and Sarah sent out Hagar and Ishmael, the Bible says that an angel ministered unto them.

> And God heard the voice of the boy, and the angel of God called to Hagar from heaven and said to her, "What troubles you, Hagar? Fear not, for God has heard the voice of the boy where he is" (Genesis 21:17 ESV).

The angel brought this good news to Hagar.

3. THREE ANGELS VISIT ABRAHAM

The Bible says that three angels, described as men, visited Abraham while on their way to Sodom. These angels appeared in the form of men.

> And the Lord appeared to him by the oaks of Mamre, as he sat at the door of his tent in the heat of the day. He lifted up his eyes and looked, and behold, three men were standing in front of him. When he saw them, he ran from the tent door to meet them and bowed himself to the earth (Genesis 18:1,2 ESV).

The angels who met Abraham included the "angel of the LORD."

4. ANGELS RESCUED LOT FROM SODOM

Two of these angels rescued Lot from the destruction of Sodom. The Book of Genesis reports it as follows.

> When he hesitated, the men grabbed him, his wife, and his two daughters by their hands, because the LORD wanted to spare Lot. They brought them safely outside the city (Genesis 19:16 God's Word).

These angelic messengers rescued Lot from the evil city of Sodom immediately before it was to be destroyed.

5. JACOB ENCOUNTERED ANGELS

Jacob had a variety of experiences with angels. One of these episodes was his famous dream.

> He had a dream in which he saw a stairway resting on the earth, with its top reaching to heaven, and the angels of God were ascending and descending on it (Genesis 28:12 NIV).

An angel appeared to Jacob in another dream.

> The angel of God said to me in the dream, 'Jacob.' I answered, 'Here I am' (Genesis 31:11 NIV).

Later, angels met Jacob as he traveled.

> Jacob went on his way, and the angels of God met him. And when Jacob saw them he said, "This is God's camp!" So he called the name of that place Mahanaim (Genesis 32:1,2 ESV).

Mahanaim means "two camps."

At the end of his life, Jacob said.

> The angel who has redeemed me from all evil, bless the boys; and in them let my name be carried on, and the name of my fathers Abraham and Isaac; and let them grow into a multitude in the midst of the earth (Genesis 48:16 ESV).

Jacob, therefore, had a number of experiences with angels.

6. THERE WAS A PASSOVER ANGEL

The angel of death killed every firstborn, of both humans and animals, of those families who did not have blood placed over the door post. The families of those who placed the blood were passed over; they were not punished (Exodus 12).

7. THEY WERE PRESENT AT THE GIVING OF THE LAW

Angels were also present at the giving of the law. We read about this in the Book of Deuteronomy.

> He said, "The LORD came from Sinai. For his people he rose from Seir like the sun. He appeared like sunshine from Mount Paran. He came with tens of thousands of holy ones. On his right was a raging fire for them" (Deuteronomy 33:2 God's Word).

The psalmist also wrote.

> With mighty chariotry, twice ten thousand, thousands upon thousands, the Lord came from Sinai into the holy place (Psalm 68:17 NRSV).

The "mighty chariotry" is a term for angels. Here they are described as innumerable.

ANGELS WERE INVOLVED IN THE GIVING OF THE LAW

In the speech of Stephen, before he suffered a martyr's death, angels are acknowledged as being directly involved when God gave the law to Moses.

> "This Moses, whom they rejected, saying, 'Who made you a ruler and a judge?'—this man God sent as both ruler and redeemer by the hand of the angel who appeared to him in the bush. . . This is the one who was in the congregation in the wilderness with the angel who spoke to him at Mount Sinai, and with our fathers. He received living oracles to give to us . . you who received the law as delivered by angels and did not keep it (Acts 7:35,38,53 ESV).

Paul also emphasized this when he wrote the following to the Galatians. He put it this way.

114

Why then the law? It was added because of transgressions, until the offspring should come to whom the promise had been made, and it was put in place through angels by an intermediary (Galatians 3:19 ESV).

The writer to the Hebrews concurred with this. He wrote these words.

For since the message declared by angels proved to be reliable, and every transgression or disobedience received a just retribution, how shall we escape if we neglect such a great salvation? It was declared at first by the Lord, and it was attested to us by those who heard (Hebrews 2:2,3 ESV).

In some sense, angels delivered the law to the people of Israel. It seems that the Lord instructed angels who, in turn, instructed Moses when the law was given. While we may not know what their specific involvement may have been, the point is that God used them to deliver His law to the people. In other words, they played an important role.

8. AN ANGEL GAVE A WARNING TO BALAAM

God sent His angel to warn the Gentile prophet Balaam that he was disobeying the Lord. In the Book of Numbers, it says the following.

"But I am the same donkey you always ride on," the donkey answered. "Have I ever done anything like this before?" "No," he admitted. Then the LORD opened Balaam's eyes, and he saw the angel of the LORD standing in the roadway with a drawn sword in his hand. Balaam fell face down on the ground before him (Numbers 22:30,31 NLT).

On this occasion, the angel of the Lord stopped Balaam.

9. AN ANGEL REBUKED ISRAEL

An angel rebuked Israel for their idolatry. We read about this in the Book of Judges.

Now the angel of the Lord went up from Gilgal to Bochim. And he said, "I brought you up from Egypt and brought you into the land that I swore to give to your fathers. I said, 'I will never break my covenant with you, and you shall make no covenant with the inhabitants of this land; you shall break down their altars.' But you have not obeyed my voice. What is this you have done? So now I say, I will not drive them out before you, but they shall become thorns in your sides, and their gods shall be a snare to you." As soon as the angel of the Lord spoke these words to all the people of Israel, the people lifted up their voices and wept (Judges 2:1-4 ESV).

The angel was sent to rebuke the sinning nation. This is another instance of the meaning of the term angel, "messenger." Indeed, this heavenly messenger delivered God's truth to the people causing them to intensely cry because of their sin.

10. AN ANGEL CURSED THE ENEMIES OF THE LORD

During the time of the Judges, an angel cursed those who did not help the Lord against His enemies. We read of this as follows.

"Curse Meroz!" said the Messenger of the LORD. "Bitterly curse those who live there! They did not come to help the LORD, to help the LORD and his heroes" (Judges 5:23 God's Word).

This angel of the Lord cursed the enemies of the God of Israel. The idea, that those who oppose the Lord are cursed, is a consistent theme throughout Scripture. Indeed, unless they repent a horrific punishment awaits them.

11. THEY JUDGED ISRAEL FOR DAVID'S SIN

When David sinned by numbering the people of Israel, God judged them through the angel of the LORD. We read about this in Samuel.

And when the angel stretched out his hand toward Jerusalem
to destroy it, the Lord relented from the calamity and said to
the angel who was working destruction among the people,
"It is enough; now stay your hand." And the angel of the
Lord was by the threshing floor of Araunah the Jebusite.
Then David spoke to the Lord when he saw the angel who
was striking the people, and said, "Behold, I have sinned,
and I have done wickedly. But these sheep, what have they
done? Please let your hand be against me and against my
father's house (2 Samuel 24:16-17 ESV).

The sin of David caused the people of Israel to be judged. Yet all was
not lost. Note that the angel was by the threshing floor of Araunah the
Jebusite when the Lord stopped this judgment of the people.

This site would later become the location of the temple which Solomon,
David's son would build. It would be the place where the Lord would
symbolically dwell among His people. It will also play a huge part in the
future events of this planet (see our book *The Jews, Jerusalem, and the
Coming Temple*). Therefore, in God's judgment, we also see His mercy.

12. ELIJAH WAS STRENGTHENED BY AN ANGEL

The prophet Elijah was strengthened by an angel who brought him
things to eat and drink. We read about this in the Book of First Kings.

Then he lay down and slept under the broom plant. An angel
touched him and said, "Get up and eat." When he looked, he
saw near his head some bread baked on hot stones and a jar
of water. So he ate, drank, and went to sleep again. The angel
of the LORD came back and woke him up again. The angel
said, "Get up and eat, or your journey will be too much for
you" (1 Kings 19:5-7 God's Word).

God used an angel, one of His messengers, to strengthen the prophet.
This illustrates what the writer to the Hebrews would later say about
their ministry.

Are not all angels ministering spirits sent to serve those who will inherit salvation (Hebrews 1:14 NIV).

Angels are indeed sent to serve those of us who have inherited the salvation of the Lord.

13. AN ANGEL KILLED THE ASSYRIANS

The angel of the LORD killed a large number of the Assyrian army. The Book of Kings records the event in this manner.

> And that night the angel of the Lord went out and struck down 185,000 in the camp of the Assyrians. And when people arose early in the morning, behold, these were all dead bodies. Then Sennacherib king of Assyria departed and went home and lived at Nineveh. And as he was worshiping in the house of Nisroch his god, Adrammelech and Sharezer, his sons, struck him down with the sword and escaped into the land of Ararat. And Esarhaddon his son reigned in his place (2 Kings 19:35-37 ESV).

These Assyrians were killed by the angel of the Lord in their attempt to conquer the city of Jerusalem.

Interestingly, we know from some of the ancient monuments of Assyria that Jerusalem was not conquered when they invaded Israel at this time in history. This omission in their records is a silent testimony to this episode.

14. AN ANGEL SAVED THREE HEBREWS FROM THE FIERY FURNACE

The three friends of Daniel—Hananiah, Mishael, and Azariah— were saved from the fiery furnace by an angel. King Nebuchadnezzar described what he saw as follows.

> He answered and said, "But I see four men unbound, walking in the midst of the fire, and they are not hurt; and the appearance of the fourth is like a son of the gods" (Daniel 3:25 ESV).

Nebuchadnezzar used the pagan phrase "like a son of the gods" to describe the fourth man. In reality, God used a heavenly messenger to rescue the three young Hebrews from certain death. Again, the Lord was there to help His people by means of an angel.

15. AN ANGEL PRESERVED THE LIFE OF DANIEL

An angel preserved the life of the prophet Daniel in the lion's den. Daniel himself testified to this as follows.

> My God sent his angel and shut the lions' mouths, and they have not harmed me, because I was found blameless before him; and also before you, O king, I have done no harm (Daniel 6:22 ESV).

The angel supernaturally kept Daniel from being eaten by the lions.

To sum up, the Old Testament gives us numerous examples of angels doing the work of the Lord. They served Him from the beginning of creation as well as throughout the entire history of nation of Israel.

SUMMARY TO QUESTION 17
WHAT HAVE ANGELS DONE ACCORDING TO THE OLD TESTAMENT?

We find that angels were very active during the period of the Old Testament. From the very beginning in the Book of Genesis, through the Babylonian captivity, they have been carrying out God's will toward humanity.

As can be seen from the biblical examples we have cited, they have appeared at crucial times in Old Testament history. Some of the more important episodes are as follows.

For example, angels were present at creation. They were there at the very beginning. The first mention of angels helping people is with Hagar, the mother of Abraham's child Ishmael.

We then find angels involved in the lives of Abraham, Lot, and Jacob. When the children of Israel were about to leave Egypt in the Exodus, the Lord sent a Passover angel to slay the firstborn of man and beast of the Egyptians. This resulted in Israel's deliverance from Egypt.

Angels were also involved at the giving of the Law at Mt. Sinai. The Bible also records an angel warning the Gentile prophet Balaam.

In the Book of Judges an angel rebuked the nation Israel for their idolatry. In another instance, an angel cursed those who did not help the Lord's people Israel.

Scripture says that God judged Israel by means of an angel because of the sin of King David. The Lord stopped the angel when he was at the location of the threshing floor of Araunah the Jebusite. This would later be the exact place where the first and second temple would be built in the city of Jerusalem.

The prophet Elijah was sustained by an angel when he was running for his life. We also discover that the Lord used a mighty angel to destroy the Assyrian army when they had sieged the city of Jerusalem.

The Book of Daniel tells us that the Lord used His angel to deliver the three Hebrew men from the fiery furnace. It was also an angel who preserved the life of Daniel when he was thrown into the den of lions.

These are some of the many appearances of angels which the Old Testament records. It is clear that the work of the Lord was sometimes carried out through angels during this period of history.

These episodes illustrate that the ministry of angels consists of doing the work of the Lord, in particular helping God's people in time of need.

In fact, each time they intervened it was for a specific purpose which always furthered the plan and purpose of God.

What Did Angels Do In The Life And Ministry Of Christ?

As angels were actively ministering during the Old Testament period, the same can be said for life of Jesus Christ. In fact, the New Testament stresses the fact that angels were observers of the ministry of Christ.

> And most certainly, the mystery of godliness is great: He was manifested in the flesh, vindicated in the Spirit, seen by angels, preached among the nations, believed on in the world, taken up in glory (1 Timothy 3:16 HCSB).

Not only was the Lord observed by angels, they appeared at various times during His time here upon the earth.

1. AN ANGEL PREDICTED HIS BIRTH

To begin with, the angel Gabriel predicted the birth of Christ to His mother Mary. We read of this occurring in the gospel of Luke. It says.

> The angel said to her, "Do not be afraid, Mary, for you have found favor with God. And now, you will conceive in your womb and bear a son, and you will name him Jesus. He will be great, and will be called the Son of the Most High, and the Lord God will give to him the throne of his ancestor David. He will reign over the house of Jacob forever, and of his kingdom there will be no end" (Luke 1:30-33 NRSV).

This important event, the birth of Christ, necessitated an angel making the announcement.

2. THEY WERE PRESENT AT HIS BIRTH

Angels were also present at the birth of Christ. Luke records this occurring. The Bible says.

> Suddenly there was a multitude of the heavenly host with the angel, praising God and saying: Glory to God in the highest heaven, and peace on earth to people He favors! (Luke 2:13,14 HCSB).

The New Living Translation says.

> Suddenly, the angel was joined by a vast host of others—the armies of heaven—praising God: "Glory to God in the highest heaven, and peace on earth to all whom God favors" (Luke 2:13,14 NLT).

Again, angels appeared at this important event. Therefore, we find a celebration of the angelic host at the time the Lord was born.

3. AN ANGEL WARNED JOSEPH TO FLEE FROM HEROD TO EGYPT

Shortly after His birth, an angel warned Joseph about Herod's plot to kill the baby Jesus. Matthew records it as follows.

> After they were gone, an angel of the Lord suddenly appeared to Joseph in a dream, saying, "Get up! Take the child and His mother, flee to Egypt, and stay there until I tell you. For Herod is about to search for the child to destroy Him" (Matthew 2:13 HCSB).

Herod wanted the Christ Child killed. The warning of the angel to Joseph caused him to take the baby Jesus, and His mother Mary, and flee to Egypt. Therefore, the life of Jesus was spared because of the warning of the angel.

4. AN ANGEL TOLD JOSEPH THAT HEROD WAS DEAD

After Herod died, an angel told Joseph to return from Egypt. We read in Matthew.

> When Herod died, an angel of the Lord suddenly appeared in a dream to Joseph in Egypt and said, "Get up, take the child and his mother, and go to the land of Israel, for those who were seeking the child's life are dead" (Matthew 2:19,20 NRSV).

The message of Herod's death was brought by an angel. This allowed the Holy Family to return to the Promised Land.

5. THEY WERE AT THE TEMPTATION OF CHRIST

In the first recorded instance of angels helping Jesus, when He had grown to be an adult, we find them ministering to Him after His temptation by the devil. This is recorded in Matthew's gospel. It says.

> Then the Devil left Him, and immediately angels came and began to serve Him (Matthew 4:11 HCSB).

Jesus was helped by angels after His forty-day temptation by the devil. This occurred after His baptism, but before the Lord began His public ministry.

ANGELS ARE NOT MENTIONED DURING JESUS' PUBLIC MINISTRY

What is conspicuous by its absence is that during the public ministry of Jesus angels are nowhere to be found. Indeed, as the Son of God, angelic help were not necessary.

6. AN ANGEL WAS WITH JESUS AT GETHSEMANE

However, after His public ministry was over, when Christ was praying at the Garden of Gethsemane while waiting to be betrayed by Judas Iscariot, an angel was there ministering to Him. Luke records what occurred.

Then an angel appeared to Him from heaven, strengthening Him (Luke 22:43 NKJV).

Again, we find an angel available to help Jesus. Interestingly, we find angels helping Him immediately before He began His public ministry and then immediately after His ministry was completed. As we just mentioned, it seems that during His ministry the help of angels was not necessary.

7. ANGELS WERE READY TO HELP AT BETRAYAL

While angels did not intervene during His public ministry, they were ready to help when Jesus was betrayed. In fact, our Lord made a point of this. He said.

Don't you realize that I could ask my Father for thousands of angels to protect us, and he would send them instantly? (Matthew 26:53 NLT).

Jesus realized that angels were available to help Him if necessary. Yet He did not call upon them. Indeed, it was not God's purpose for them to rescue Him from what He was about to experience.

8. AN ANGEL ROLLED THE STONE FROM THE TOMB

On Easter Sunday, resurrection day, an angel rolled back the stone from the tomb of Joseph of Arimathea. The Bible says.

Suddenly, there was a powerful earthquake. An angel of the Lord had come down from heaven, rolled the stone away, and was sitting on it (Matthew 28:2 God's Word).

The angel was responsible for letting people into the tomb to see that Christ had risen. It was not to let Jesus out of the tomb for He had already risen from the dead. Indeed, He supernaturally left the place where He was buried in His resurrected body.

9. AN ANGEL ANNOUNCED THE RESURRECTION OF CHRIST

An angel then announced the resurrection of Christ to the women who arrived at His tomb.

> But the angel answered and said to the women, "Do not be afraid, for I know that you seek Jesus who was crucified. He is not here; for He is risen, as He said. Come, see the place where the Lord lay" (Matthew 28:5,6 NKJV).

The fact that Jesus was raised from the dead was first announced by angels.

10. ANGELS WAS AT JESUS' ASCENSION

When Christ left this earth and ascended into heaven, there were angels present. The Book of Acts records this event. It says.

> While he was going and they were gazing up toward heaven, suddenly two men in white robes stood by them (Acts 1:10 NRSV).

When Jesus ascended, angels were there. In fact, they gave some very specific instructions to His disciples.

> They were looking intently up into the sky as he was going, when suddenly two men dressed in white stood beside them. "Men of Galilee," they said, "why do you stand here looking into the sky? This same Jesus, who has been taken from you into heaven, will come back in the same way you have seen him go into heaven (Acts 1:10-11 NIV).

The disciples were commanded to stop standing there and gazing into heaven. Indeed, there was the work of the ministry to be accomplished!

11. THERE WILL BE ANGELS AT THE SECOND COMING OF CHRIST

The Bible says angels will be with Christ at His Second Coming. In one of His parables, the wheat and the weeds, Jesus taught that the angels would pull up the weeds, the unbelievers, at the time of His return.

> As the weeds are pulled up and burned in the fire, so it will be at the end of the age. The Son of Man will send out his angels, and they will weed out of his kingdom everything that causes sin and all who do evil. They will throw them into the blazing furnace, where there will be weeping and gnashing of teeth. Then the righteous will shine like the sun in the kingdom of their Father. Whoever has ears, let them hear (Matthew 13:40-43 NIV).

Jesus also made this clear when He later spoke of the judgment of the nations. Matthew records Him saying the following.

> And He will send His angels with a great sound of a trumpet, and they will gather together His elect from the four winds, from one end of heaven to the other (Matthew 24:31 NKJV).

God will also use angels to gather believers when Christ returns to the earth.

12. THEY WILL EXECUTE CHRIST'S JUDGMENT

When the Lord comes again, angels will execute His judgment. Paul wrote.

> And God will provide rest for you who are being persecuted and also for us when the Lord Jesus appears from heaven. He will come with his mighty angels (2 Thessalonians 1:7 NLT).

Angels will be God's instruments in the divine judgment against unbelieving humanity.

13. ANGELS WILL HEAR CHRIST ACKNOWLEDGING OR DENYING PEOPLE

After the separation of the unrighteous from the righteous at the coming of Christ, the Bible says that angels will hear the Lord either acknowledging or denying each person.

> And I say to you, anyone who acknowledges Me before men, the Son of Man will also acknowledge him before the angels of God (Luke 12:8 HCSB).

Those who acknowledge Christ will be acknowledged in the presence of His angels.

14. ANGELS SAW JESUS IN HIS DEITY AND HUMANITY

It is important to remember that angels had seen Jesus, as God the Son, previously to Him becoming a man. When Jesus humbled Himself in becoming human, they saw the Lord of the universe make Himself into a servant.

These same angels, who had seen God the Son banish the created spirit-being who became the devil after the original rebellion, observed this same evil personage tempting Jesus.

The angels also saw Jesus suffering at the hands of sinful humanity, agonizing in the Garden of Gethsemane, and dying a humiliating death between two criminals. Indeed, they observed the great love that Jesus showed toward humanity.

In sum, angels were present as participants, as well as observers, throughout the entire ministry of Jesus Christ upon the earth.

SUMMARY TO QUESTION 18
WHAT DID ANGELS DO IN THE LIFE AND MINISTRY OF CHRIST?

Angels can be found throughout the life of Jesus Christ. From His birth, to His ascension into heaven, angels played an important role in the life of Christ.

The Bible says that the angels predicted His birth to Joseph and Mary. They were also present when He was born. An angel then warned Joseph about those who were attempting to kill the baby Jesus. The life of the child was saved as the family fled to Egypt. An angel later informed Joseph when the evil King Herod had died so they could return to the land.

Before His public ministry began, we find that angels ministered to Jesus after His temptation. When His public ministry had ended, angels were there to strengthen Jesus in the Garden of Gethsemane. Angels were also ready to help Jesus when Judas betrayed Him.

While angels were present immediately before His public ministry began as well as immediately after it was over, they are nowhere to be found during the three plus years that the Lord ministered here upon the earth. The fact that they were not active participants in His life and ministry is significant. Indeed, they were not necessary for Him to accomplish His mission.

After His death, the Bible says an angel rolled the stone away from the tomb of Jesus on the day of His resurrection. When Jesus ascended into heaven angels were present. Indeed, they gave instructions to His disciples to stop gazing into heaven and begin the work of the ministry!

Angels will be with Christ at His Second Coming. They will execute His judgment. In fact, we are told that angels will separate the righteous from unrighteous. They will first gather the unbelievers and bring them to judgment, then they will gather the righteous who are here upon the earth.

In sum, just as angels surround the throne of God the Father and serve Him, they also were around Jesus—attending to the needs of God the Son, when it was necessary.

What Ministry Did The Angels Have In The Early Church?

Angels were busy ministering to people after the time of Christ. In fact, as we look at the history of the early church, we find angels helping God's people in various ways.

1. AN ANGEL APPEARED TO PHILIP

An angel appeared to Philip and directed him toward the Ethiopian eunuch. We read of this in the Book of Acts.

> An angel of the Lord spoke to Philip: "Get up and go south to the road that goes down from Jerusalem to Gaza." (This is the desert road.) (Acts 8:26 HCSB).

The Lord saw the need to send an angel to direct Philip to preach the gospel to a particular individual; the Ethiopian eunuch.

2. AN ANGEL APPEARED TO CORNELIUS

When a Gentile believer named Cornelius wanted to know more about the Lord, an angel was sent to him.

> In Caesarea there was a man named Cornelius, a centurion of the Italian Cohort, as it was called. He was a devout man who feared God with all his household; he gave alms generously to the people and prayed constantly to God. One

afternoon at about three o'clock he had a vision in which he clearly saw an angel of God coming in and saying to him, "Cornelius" (Acts 10:1-3 NRSV).

We find an angel coming to Cornelius as an answer to his prayer. The angel instructed Cornelius to send for Simon Peter who would tell him the message of Jesus the Christ. This opened the door for Gentiles, non-Jews, to become part of the family of believers, the church.

3. PETER WAS HELPED OUT OF JAIL BY AN ANGEL

The Bible says that an angel supernaturally helped get the Apostle Peter out of jail. We read of this in the Book of Acts where it says the following.

> When Peter came to his senses, he said, "Now I'm sure that the Lord sent his angel to rescue me from Herod and from everything the Jewish people are expecting to happen to me" (Acts 12:11 God's Word).

Peter's escape came as a result of the divine work of an angel.

4. HEROD WAS KILLED BY AN ANGEL

The evil king Herod was killed by an angel of the Lord. The Book of Acts says.

> Instantly, an angel of the Lord struck Herod with a sickness, because he accepted the people's worship instead of giving the glory to God. So he was consumed with worms and died (Acts 12:23 NLT).

The Lord used an angel to punish this evil king.

5. AN ANGEL ENCOURAGED PAUL

When Paul faced a storm at sea on his way to Rome, the Lord sent an angel to encourage him. Paul told the people on the ship what had happened.

For this very night there stood before me an angel of the God
to whom I belong and whom I worship, and he said, 'Do not
be afraid, Paul; you must stand before Caesar. And behold,
God has granted you all those who sail with you.' So take
heart, men, for I have faith in God that it will be exactly as
I have been told. But we must run aground on some island
(Acts 27:23-26 ESV).

The angel who visited Paul reassured him that all on the ship would be
saved. As always, the Word of God came true, all were indeed saved.

THE CHURCH TESTIFIES TO ANGELS AND OTHER HEAVENLY BEINGS

We have seen that angels ministered to certain believers in the early
church. In the same manner, the Bible says that the church unveiled
God's wisdom to the angels.

God's purpose was to show his wisdom in all its rich variety
to all the rulers and authorities in the heavenly realms. They
will see this when Jews and Gentiles are joined together in
his church (Ephesians 3:10 NLT).

Angels, as well as other specially created beings, observed the wisdom
and purpose of God when Jews and Gentiles became part of one body,
one family, the church.

Consequently, we find angels at work during crucial times when the
gospel was being spread. In addition, God's ministry in bringing both
Jews and Gentiles into the church was a testimony to the angels as well
as to all the other spirit-beings the Lord had created.

SUMMARY TO QUESTION 19
WHAT MINISTRY DID THE ANGELS HAVE IN THE EARLY CHURCH?

The ministry of angels did not stop with the ascension of Jesus into
heaven. During its early period, when the New Testament church was

growing, we find angels ministering to God's people. The Book of Acts, which chronicles the beginning of the church, lists five different appearances of angels to His people.

Phillip the evangelist was specially directed by an angel. He was led to speak the message of Jesus to a certain eunuch on his way back to Ethiopia. The man responded to Philip's message about the Lord and became a believer in Christ.

An angel appeared to Cornelius, the Gentile centurion, with the message that his prayers had been answered. Soon thereafter Cornelius and his family heard the good news about Jesus Christ from Simon Peter. They listened and believed. This opened the door for Gentiles, non-Jews, to be part of God's family of believers, the church.

In the city of Jerusalem, the Apostle Peter was set free from his chains in prison by an angel of the Lord. The angel then supernaturally led Peter to safety.

An angel killed the evil king Herod who publicly glorified himself instead of glorifying God. In this case, the angel was used to carry out God's punishment.

Finally, the Apostle Paul was encouraged by an angel when facing a terrible storm at sea. This angelic personage showed Paul that the people on the ship would survive. True to this promise, all of the people did survive.

In writing to the Ephesians Paul emphasized the church itself is a testimony to angels of the wisdom of God. The specific events recorded in the Book of Acts which involved angels certainly testify to this truth. As in other times in biblical history, the Lord used angels to do His bidding.

QUESTION 20

What Will Angels Do According To The Book Of Revelation?

Angels are at work from the first pages of the Scripture until the last. According to the Book of Revelation, the last book of the Bible, there will be a future ministry of angels. Their work toward God and humanity is not yet finished. The evidence is as follows.

1. COUNTLESS NUMBER OF ANGELS WORSHIP GOD

We find that there are innumerable angels worshipping around God's throne with the "living creatures" as well as the "elders;" who may or may not be heavenly beings. We read the following account of this occurring.

> Then I looked, and I heard the voice of many angels surrounding the throne and the living creatures and the elders; they numbered myriads of myriads and thousands of thousands (Revelation 5:11 ESV).

All of these godly spirit-beings were found worshipping the living God, day and night.

2. FOUR ANGELS RESTRAIN THE WINDS

The Bible says four angels will restrain the winds upon the earth. Scripture says.

After this I saw four angels standing at the four corners of the earth. They were holding back the four winds of the earth to keep them from blowing on the land, the sea, or any tree (Revelation 7:1 God's Word).

These angels will miraculously cause the winds to stop blowing.

3. SEVEN ANGELS SOUND SEVEN TRUMPETS OF JUDGMENT

There will be seven angels that will stand before the Lord with seven trumpets. John wrote.

And I saw the seven angels who stand before God, and seven trumpets were given to them (Revelation 8:2 ESV).

They sound the trumpets of judgment. This will occur during the time leading up to the Second Coming of Christ.

4. ANGELS WILL FIGHT ALONGSIDE MICHAEL

Angels will be fighting in heaven under the leadership of Michael the archangel. The Bible says that they will fight with the dragon, the devil, and his evil angels.

Now war arose in heaven, Michael and his angels fighting against the dragon. And the dragon and his angels fought back, but he was defeated, and there was no longer any place for them in heaven. And the great dragon was thrown down, that ancient serpent, who is called the devil and Satan, the deceiver of the whole world— he was thrown down to the earth, and his angels were thrown down with him. And I heard a loud voice in heaven, saying, "Now the salvation and the power and the kingdom of our God and the authority of his Christ have come, for the accuser of our brothers has been thrown down, who accuses them day and night before our God" (Revelation 12:7-10 ESV).

Evil angels will be at war with Michael, and the righteous angels. As the Bible notes, the good angels will prevail.

5. AN ANGEL WILL PREACH THE MESSAGE OF CHRIST TO THE ENTIRE WORLD

Before the end comes, an angel will travel all around the world and preach the good news about Christ to those who remain on the earth. The Scripture puts it this way.

> Then I saw another angel flying directly overhead, with an eternal gospel to proclaim to those who dwell on earth, to every nation and tribe and language and people. And he said with a loud voice, "Fear God and give him glory, because the hour of his judgment has come, and worship him who made heaven and earth, the sea and the springs of water (Revelation 14:6,7 ESV).

The message of Christ is preached worldwide by an angel. Every language group upon the face of the earth will receive this message.

6. AN ANGEL WILL ANNOUNCE THE FALL OF BABYLON

An angel will announce the fall of the city of Babylon. John wrote.

> Another angel, a second one, followed him, and said, "Fallen! Babylon the Great has fallen! She has made all the nations drink the wine of her passionate sexual sins" (Revelation 14:8 God's Word).

When Babylon falls, it will be announced by an angel.

7. THE WICKED ARE PUNISHED BEFORE ANGELS

The wicked will be punished in the presence of the holy angels. We read.

And another angel, a third, followed them, saying with a
loud voice, "If anyone worships the beast and its image and
receives a mark on his forehead or on his hand, he also will
drink the wine of God's wrath, poured full strength into the
cup of his anger, and he will be tormented with fire and sul-
fur in the presence of the holy angels and in the presence of
the Lamb" (Revelation 14:9,10 ESV).

Those who take the "mark of the beast" will punished in front of the
angels of God.

8. THEY ARE HARVESTERS AT THE END OF THE AGE

God will send the angels to become harvesters at the end time. They
will harvest both the good and the evil.

Another angel came out of the temple in heaven. He, too,
had a sharp sickle. Yet another angel came from the altar
with authority over fire. This angel called out in a loud voice
to the angel with the sharp sickle, "Swing your sickle, and
gather the bunches of grapes from the vine of the earth,
because those grapes are ripe." The angel swung his sickle
on the earth and gathered the grapes from the vine of the
earth. He threw them into the winepress of God's anger
(Revelation 14:17-19 God's Word).

Jesus also spoke of angels coming at the end-time harvest
to separate the righteous from the unrighteous (Matthew
13:24-30).

9. ANGELS WILL POUR OUT BOWLS OF JUDGMENT

Before Jesus Christ returns, angels will pour out seven bowls of judgment upon the people of the earth (Revelation 15 and 16).

10. AN ANGEL REVEALS THE GREAT PROSTITUTE TO JOHN

The great prostitute of Babylon is revealed to John by an angel (Revelation 17:1-7). Again, an angel figures prominently in the events of the Book of Revelation.

11. AN ANGEL CALLS FOR PUNISHMENT

John saw an angel calling for the punishment of the unbelieving people on the earth. John wrote.

> Then I saw an angel standing in the sun, and with a loud voice he called to all the birds that fly directly overhead, "Come, gather for the great supper of God" (Revelation 19:17 ESV).

Punishment is called for by an angel.

12. AN ANGEL BINDS SATAN AND SENDS HIM TO THE ABYSS

After Jesus Christ returns, an angel will bind Satan in the abyss, the bottomless pit, for a thousand years. We read the following in the Book of Revelation.

> I saw an angel coming down from heaven, holding the key to the bottomless pit and a large chain in his hand. He over-powered the serpent, that ancient snake, named Devil and Satan. The angel chained up the serpent for 1,000 years. He threw it into the bottomless pit. The angel shut and sealed the pit over the serpent to keep it from deceiving the nations anymore until the 1,000 years were over. After that it must be set free for a little while (Revelation 20:1-3 God's Word).

We find that God uses an angel to bind Satan.

13. THERE IS NO MENTION OF ANGELIC MINISTRY IN THE KINGDOM AGE

According to the premillennial view of the future, Jesus Christ will rule as the King of Kings in His visible glory upon the earth for one thousand years. After that time the eternal state will begin. Interestingly, there is no mention of any angelic ministry during the millennial reign of Christ. This is similar to the public ministry of Jesus where no angels were involved.

There is the viewpoint among some Bible-believers that there will be no literal thousand-year reign of Christ upon the earth in the future. According to this position, when Christ returns the eternal state will begin without any intervening period.

14. ANGELS PRAISE GOD IN THE ETERNAL STATE

In the eternal state we will find the angels praising God. The Bible says the following.

> But you have come to Mount Zion and to the city of the living God, the heavenly Jerusalem, and to innumerable angels in festal gathering, and to the assembly of the firstborn who are enrolled in heaven, and to God, the judge of all, and to the spirits of the righteous made perfect, and to Jesus, the mediator of a new covenant, and to the sprinkled blood that speaks a better word than the blood of Abel (Hebrews 12:22-24 ESV).

Angels will praise God for all eternity.

Thus, we find that the Book of Revelation continues the story of God's worked being performed by angels.

SUMMARY TO QUESTION 20
WHAT WILL ANGELS DO ACCORDING TO THE BOOK OF REVELATION?

Angels have always played a role in carrying out the plan of God on the earth. Therefore, it is not surprising that we find them at work numerous times in the last book of the Bible, the Book of Revelation. Indeed, we discover that angels play a prominent role in this particular book. They include the following.

To begin with, it was an angel who revealed the contents of the Book of Revelation to John the apostle. The book is a revelation about Jesus Christ, delivered through the means of an angel.

Revelation testifies that there are countless numbers of living creatures, including angels, who are before the throne of God constantly worshipping Him.

During the time of God's judgment, four angels will be sent to actually restrain the amount of damage done to the earth and its inhabitants.

The trumpets of judgment which are sounded to signify God's wrath on sinful humanity are sounded by angels.

Scripture speaks of an angelic war in heaven led by Michael the archangel. In this war, he fights with the devil and his angels. The result is that the devil and his evil angels are kicked out of heaven.

We also find an angel proclaiming God's message to the world. This particular angel goes around the entire earth proclaiming the everlasting gospel in every language.

There is another angel who announces the fall of Babylon.

The Bible also says that the wicked will be judged in the presence of God's holy angels. At the end of the age, the angels will appear like harvesters, separating the righteous from the evil.

At the Second Coming of Jesus Christ, Scripture says that an angel binds Satan and places him in the bottomless pit for a thousand years.

Interestingly, in the Book of Revelation there is no direct mention of the role of angels in the kingdom age; the time Christ rules the world after His Second Coming. This is similar to what we have discovered about the public ministry of Jesus, angels were not involved during the entire time He ministered.

However, we do find that angels will be praising God in the eternal state.

Therefore, the Book of Revelation, the last Book of the Bible, is in harmony with the rest of Scripture. Indeed, it testifies that angels will have a future role in the plan of God.

QUESTION 21

Who Is Michael
The Archangel?

One of the most prominent characters in the Bible is Michael the "archangel," or "chief angel." He is the only angel specifically designated as an "archangel." His name means, "who is like God?" He is mentioned a number of times in Scripture. From the Bible we know the following things about him.

1. HE IS ONE OF THE CHIEF PRINCES

Michael is called "one of the chief princes." In the Book of Daniel, we read the following.

> The prince of the kingdom of Persia withstood me twenty-one days, but Michael, one of the chief princes, came to help me, for I was left there with the kings of Persia (Daniel 10:13 ESV).

This title suggests the highest rank.

2. HE SUPPORTED ANOTHER ANGEL

Michael supported another angel who was being hindered from answering Daniel's prayer. He said to Daniel.

> But I will tell you what is inscribed in the book of truth: there is none who contends by my side against these except Michael, your prince (Daniel 10:21 ESV).

Therefore, we find that Michael has the ability to support other angels in their ministries.

3. HE WILL HAVE AN END TIMES MINISTRY

Michael will have a prominent role in the end times. We read the following in the Book of Daniel.

> The person who looked like a human continued, "At that time Michael, the great commander, will stand up on behalf of the descendants of your people. It will be a time of trouble unlike any that has existed from the time there have been nations until that time. But at that time your people, everyone written in the book, will be rescued. Many sleeping in the ground will wake up. Some will wake up to live forever, but others will wake up to be ashamed and disgraced forever. Those who are wise will shine like the brightness on the horizon. Those who lead many people to righteousness will shine like the stars forever and ever. But you, Daniel, keep these words secret, and seal the book until the end times. Many will travel everywhere, and knowledge will grow" (Daniel 12:1-4 God's Word).

According to this passage, Michael has a direct connection with the nation Israel in the "last days."

4. HE IS POSSIBLY THE ARCHANGEL MENTIONED IN 1 THESSALONIANS

Michael is thought by some to be the archangel alluded to in First Thessalonians. Paul wrote the following.

> For the Lord himself will descend from heaven with a cry of command, with the voice of an archangel, and with the sound of the trumpet of God. And the dead in Christ will rise first (1 Thessalonians 4:16 ESV).

While the identity of this chief angel is not stated, it could possibly be Michael. However, it is also likely that the voice referred to here is not the voice of the archangel, but actually the voice of the Lord Himself. His voice is powerful, it is like that of an archangel.

5. HE DISPUTED WITH SATAN OVER MOSES' BODY

We are told that Michael contended with Satan over the body of Moses. Jude wrote about an episode which is not contained in the Old Testament.

> But even the archangel Michael, when he was disputing with the devil about the body of Moses, did not dare to bring a slanderous accusation against him, but said, "The Lord rebuke you!" (Jude 9, NIV).

This is the only passage where Michael is specifically called an archangel. The New Living Translation puts it this way.

> But even Michael, one of the mightiest of the angels, did not dare accuse Satan of blasphemy, but simply said, "The Lord rebuke you." (This took place when Michael was arguing with Satan about Moses' body) (Jude 9 NLT).

Interestingly, we find that Michael did not rebuke the devil on his own but rather called upon the name of the Lord to rebuke him.

6. HE WILL WAR AGAINST SATAN

Before Jesus Christ comes back, Michael and his angels will engage in a war with Satan and his angels. We read the following in the Book of Revelation.

> Then war broke out in heaven. Michael and his angels fought against the dragon, and the dragon and his angels fought back. But he was not strong enough, and they lost their place in heaven. The great dragon was hurled down—that ancient serpent called the devil, or Satan, who leads the whole world astray. He was hurled to the earth, and his angels with him (Revelation 12:7-9 NIV).

143

Michael and his army will prevail and Satan will be thrown down to the earth.

7. HE IS THE MESSENGER OF LAW AND JUDGMENT

After looking at what the totality of Scripture has to say about Michael the archangel, he seems to be the messenger of law and judgment.

This sums up the specific passages in Scripture where Michael the archangel appears. As we have seen, he is prominent in carrying out God's program both here on earth as well as in the heavenly realm.

SUMMARY TO QUESTION 21
WHO IS MICHAEL THE ARCHANGEL?

There is much confusion about the identity and ministry of Michael the archangel. From looking at the Scripture, we can conclude the following about this personage.

He is the only archangel specifically named in Scripture. No other angel is given this title. However, since Michael is called the "one of chief princes" there are obviously other angels of this rank. Yet none of them are named.

His authority and rank is seen by the fact that he actually supports another angel in spiritual warfare. Michael is obviously a powerful being.

Daniel the prophet wrote that Michael will have a prominent role in the end times. He seems to have some connection with the nation Israel and their destiny. This is also confirmed in the Book of Revelation where Michael and his angels are at war with Satan during the time of the end.

Jude records an episode which is not found in the Old Testament. It consists of Michael disputing with Satan over the body of Moses. As powerful as Michael is, he had to rebuke Satan in the name of the Lord. It seems he could not overcome him in his own strength.

This sums up the little information we have concerning Michael the archangel.

Is It Possible To Identify Michael The Archangel With Jesus?

There have been those who have attempted to equate Michael the archangel with Jesus; that they are the same person. Some feel that Michael is Jesus Christ appearing in a temporary form, such as Christ did as the angel of the Lord.

THIS IS A DIFFERENT VIEW THAN THE WATCHTOWER BIBLE AND TRACT SOCIETY – THE JEHOVAH WITNESSES

At the outset, we must note that this is different than the view of the Watchtower Bible and Tract Society, the Jehovah Witnesses. They believe that Jesus Christ is a created being who was Michael the archangel in the Old Testament; a view totally incompatible with what the Bible says about Jesus. The question we are addressing is this: was Michael actually the pre-incarnate Christ?

THE CASE FOR MICHAEL BEING JESUS

The arguments for Michael's identification as being the Pre-incarnate Christ are as follows.

1. MICHAEL IS THE CHIEF PRINCE AND PROTECTOR

Michael is called the "chief prince" of God's people. He is also called the "protector" of the people Israel. The Bible also teaches that the Lord is the one who protects or "keeps" Israel.

My help comes from the Lord, who made heaven and earth. He will not let your foot be moved; he who keeps you will not slumber. Behold, he who keeps Israel will neither slumber nor sleep. The Lord is your keeper; the Lord is your shade on your right hand. The sun shall not strike you by day, nor the moon by night (Psalm 121:2-6 ESV).

The argument goes like this: If the LORD is the One who protects or keeps Israel, and Michael is the one who is called the protector of the people, then Michael must be the LORD who is protecting the people.

2. CHRIST WILL GIVE A COMMAND LIKE AN ANGEL

The Bible says that when Christ returns, He will come with the voice, or cry of command, of the archangel.

For the Lord Himself will descend from heaven with a shout, with the voice of an archangel, and with the trumpet of God. And the dead in Christ will rise first (1 Thessalonians 4:16 NKJV).

Since Christ comes with the voice of the archangel, the argument goes that He must be that archangel. The only archangel named in Scripture is Michael.

RESPONSE TO THE ARGUMENT THAT MICHAEL IS JESUS

The biblical evidence does not substantiate the idea that Michael the archangel was actually God the Son, Jesus. The following points make this clear.

1. MICHAEL ONLY HAS AUTHORITY OVER OTHER ANGELS

The fact that Michael is called a chief prince only means that he has authority over other angels; not over everything that exists. There is no statement in Scripture that says Michael has authority over all things.

2. JESUS IS NEVER CALLED THE CHIEF PRINCE

In addition, Jesus is never called the chief prince in Scripture. To the contrary, He is the King of kings and Lord of lords.

> On his robe and thigh was written this title: King of kings and Lord of lords (Revelation 19:16 NLT).

Though Michael has protected Israel, it is as God's representative. It is ultimately the Lord, not Michael, who is protecting or "keeping" His chosen people.

3. MICHAEL IS ONE OF THE CHIEF PRINCES

In addition, Michael is called "one of the chief princes." We read the following in the Book of Daniel

> But the prince of the kingdom of Persia opposed me twenty-one days. So Michael, one of the chief princes, came to help me, and I left him there with the prince of the kingdom of Persia (Daniel 10:13 NRSV).

This means that he is one of a group of princes. We do not know how large the group is, but he is not in a class by himself. On the other hand, the Bible says that Jesus is the unique Son of God. John wrote.

> No one has ever seen God; the only God, who is at the Father's side, he has made him known (John 1:18 ESV).

Jesus is different than angels or humans, He is God the Son.

4. CHRIST COMES WITH A VOICE LIKE AN ARCHANGEL

The fact that Jesus Christ cries out with the voice, or cry of command, like an archangel does not mean that He is one. The voice He uses will be "like" or "as" that of an archangel. In other words, the Scripture is stressing that He has a powerful voice.

5. MICHAEL IS THE HIGHEST OF THE ANGELS

Michael is the highest of the angels; an order of created beings. He is one of the angels, he is not the Creator of the angels as the Bible says that Jesus is. Paul wrote the following about Christ.

> For by him all things were created, in heaven and on earth, visible and invisible, whether thrones or dominions or rulers or authorities—all things were created through him and for him (Colossians 1:16 ESV).

Again, Christ has a unique standing. Indeed, He is not in the class of angels.

6. MICHAEL WOULD NOT REBUKE THE DEVIL

There is a further problem with the identification of Jesus with Michael. The Book of Jude makes a distinction between Michael and the Lord. It says.

> But even Michael, one of the mightiest of the angels, did not dare accuse Satan of blasphemy, but simply said, "The Lord rebuke you." (This took place when Michael was arguing with Satan about Moses' body (Jude 9 NLT).

Michael is obviously not the Lord. He could not rebuke the devil on his own, but rather called upon the Lord to rebuke him.

On the other hand, Jesus has no such problem with the devil. In fact, we find that He personally rebuked him, since He is the Lord.

> Jesus answered, "Go away Satan! The Scriptures say: 'Worship the Lord your God and serve only him.'" Then the devil left Jesus, and angels came to help him (Matthew 4:10,11 CEV).

Jesus rebuked Satan, something Michael was not able to do. In doing so, Christ made it clear that only the Lord is to be worshipped. No other creatures, angel or human, should be given worship.

7. MICHAEL'S NAME BEARS TESTIMONY TO HIS CHARACTER

Michael, the one who is closest in proximity to the Lord at the top of the angelic creation, bears testimony to the great gap between the Creator and the created. His name means, "Who is like God?"

The answer, of course, is no one. The closer one gets to God, the more they realize their own nothingness and His greatness. Neither Michael, nor any of the angels, is like God.

SUMMARY TO QUESTION 22
IS IT POSSIBLE TO IDENTIFY MICHAEL THE ARCHANGEL WITH JESUS?

In the Scripture, there is a powerful angel named Michael. Some identify Michael with Jesus Christ, God the Son. They believe that God the Son appeared as an angelic messenger and took the name Michael.

This is not the same idea that Jesus is a created being, as argued by the Jehovah Witnesses, but rather the belief that Jesus, as God the Son took on angelic form with the name Michael.

Support for this belief includes the fact that Michael is called the chief prince and protector of Israel. This is an attribute that belongs to God alone.

In addition, when Christ returns to the earth He will give a shout like an archangel. This could be another indication that He and Michael are the same person.

While some people attempt to equate Michael the archangel with Jesus, there is really no biblical evidence to do this. To the contrary, Jesus and Michael are two different personages.

For one thing, Michael has authority over the angels, not over everything. He is one of God's subordinates who has been given charge of the angelic host, but nothing else. The Lord is the one who protects His people.

While Michael is called the chief prince, Jesus is never called by this title. Furthermore, Michael is called "one of the chief princes." He is not the only one. Jesus, on the other hand, is the unique Son of God.

In addition, Jesus will come to snatch away the believers with the voice of an archangel or a powerful voice. It does not say He is an archangel. Therefore, we have no identification of the two.

Michael is the highest of the angels—an order of created beings while Jesus is the uncreated Second Person of the Trinity, God the Son.

Although Michael is the highest of the angels he could not, on his own, rebuke the devil. He had to call upon the Lord to do this. Jesus had no such limitations. He Himself told Satan to leave!

Finally, Michael's name bears testimony to his identity. His name means "who is like God?" The answer is nobody, not even Michael.

We conclude that Jesus Christ, God the Son and Michael the archangel are two different personages.

QUESTION 23

Who Is The
Angel Gabriel?

Apart from Michael the archangel, the only other angel in Scripture who is specifically named is Gabriel. His name means "God is my strength," or "mighty one." Though he is not specifically called an archangel, he is a high-ranking angel. In fact, we are told that he stands in the presence of God. Furthermore, messages of the highest importance are given to him.

THE REFERENCES TO GABRIEL

The Bible gives the following references to the angel Gabriel.

1. HE GAVE UNDERSTANDING OF THE VISION TO DANIEL

Gabriel was told to explain to Daniel the meaning of a certain vision. We read the following in the Book of Daniel.

> And I heard a human voice calling out from the Ulai River, "Gabriel, tell this man the meaning of his vision" (Daniel 8:16 NLT).

Gabriel explained to Daniel about the rule of the kingdoms of Medo-Persia and Greece. He also told Daniel about the premature death of Alexander the Great.

2. HE GAVE THE PROPHECY OF CHRIST'S COMING

In another appearance, Gabriel gave Daniel the explanation of the prophecy of Christ's coming.

> Yes, while I was speaking in prayer, the man Gabriel, whom I had seen in the vision at the beginning, being caused to fly swiftly, reached me about the time of the evening offering (Daniel 9:21 NKJV).

It was a time of despair for the nation when Gabriel came to Daniel with the message of hope. His name, "God is my strength" or "mighty one," testified to the all-powerful God who was about to deliver His people from the bondage of captivity, and bring them back into the land of promise. We read him saying.

> He spoke with me, instructing me as follows "Daniel, I have now come to impart understanding to you. At the beginning of your requests a message went out, and I have come to convey it to you, for you are of great value in God's sight. Therefore consider the message and understand the vision" (Daniel 9:22,23 NET).

Gabriel then proceed to reveal the great prophecy of the seventy weeks, or seventy sevens, to Daniel.

> Seventy 'sevens' are decreed for your people and your holy city to finish transgression, to put an end to sin, to atone for wickedness, to bring in everlasting righteousness, to seal up vision and prophecy and to anoint the Most Holy Place. "Know and understand this: From the time the word goes out to restore and rebuild Jerusalem until the Anointed One, the ruler, comes, there will be seven 'sevens,' and sixty- two 'sevens. ' It will be rebuilt with streets and a trench, but in times of trouble. After the sixty-two 'sevens,' the Anointed One will be put to death and will have nothing. The people

of the ruler who will come will destroy the city and the sanctuary. The end will come like a flood: War will continue until the end, and desolations have been decreed. He will confirm a covenant with many for one 'seven. ' In the middle of the 'seven' he will put an end to sacrifice and offering. And at the temple he will set up an abomination that causes desolation, until the end that is decreed is poured out on him (Daniel 9:24-27 NIV).

This is one of the greatest prophecies in all of Holy Scripture. Indeed, it told us the exact time when the Messiah would come the first time as well as the exact time that He will come again; when a certain event takes place which is still in the future.

3. HE WAS POSSIBLY THE GLORIOUS ANGEL

It is possible that Gabriel is the unnamed, glorious, angel who interpreted the vision of Daniel in the third year of Cyrus. We read the following concerning this angel.

I looked up and there before me was a man dressed in linen, with a belt of the finest gold around his waist (Daniel 10:5 NIV).

Another unnamed angel interpreted the vision Daniel received during the reign of Belshazzar. This angel may also have been Gabriel.

So I approached one of those standing beside the throne and asked him what it all meant. He explained it to me like this (Daniel 7:16 NLT).

This glorious angel could have been Gabriel.

4. GABRIEL ANNOUNCED THE BIRTH OF JOHN THE BAPTIST

As we move to the New Testament, we find that the angel Gabriel announced the birth of John the Baptist to his father Zechariah. The Bible says.

Then there appeared to him an angel of the Lord, standing at the right side of the altar of incense. . . The angel replied, "I am Gabriel. I stand in the presence of God, and I have been sent to speak to you and to bring you this good news" (Luke 1:11,19 NRSV).

This important event necessitated the sending of Gabriel. Here he is called "an angel of the Lord" of possible "the angel of the Lord." According to Gabriel, he has an exalted position among the angels, he stands at the right hand of God.

5. HE APPEARED TO MARY (THE ANNUNCIATION)

The angel Gabriel also appeared to Mary to announce the conception of Jesus. Luke wrote.

In the sixth month, the angel Gabriel was sent by God to a town in Galilee called Nazareth, to a virgin engaged to a man named Joseph, of the house of David. The virgin's name was Mary. And [the angel] came to her and said, "Rejoice, favored woman! The Lord is with you" (Luke 1:26-28 HCSB).

He was sent there to announce the birth of Jesus, the Savior of the world.

OTHER POSSIBLE APPEARANCES AS THE ANGEL OF THE LORD

While there are only four times when Gabriel's name is specifically mentioned in the Bible, there are other occasions where he may have appeared as the angel of the LORD.

Indeed, a number of times in the New Testament, a personage called the angel of the LORD appeared. Though he is not named, it is likely that he is Gabriel; since Gabriel is designated as the angel of the LORD in Luke 1:11.

In sum, we find that Gabriel is an angel of the highest order.

SUMMARY TO QUESTION 23
WHO IS THE ANGEL GABRIEL?

Gabriel is one of only two righteous angels which are named in Scripture. He appears in both testaments. His ministry seems to be that of mercy and promise.

We know that he appeared to the prophet Daniel. In fact, it was Gabriel who explained the meaning of one of Daniel's visions to the prophet.

The great prophecy of the coming of Christ was also announced by the angel Gabriel; the prophecy of the seventy sevens.

On two other occasions in the Book of Daniel an unnamed glorious angel interpreted a vision that Daniel had received. It is possible that Gabriel was this unnamed angel.

In the New Testament, we find Gabriel appearing to Zechariah, the father of John the Baptist. He announced that Zechariah and his wife Elizabeth would conceive a son in their old age. In this episode, Gabriel also identified himself as the angel who stands at the right hand of God.

Soon after the appearance to Zechariah, Gabriel appeared to Mary, the mother of Jesus, announcing the conception and future birth of the Christ Child.

Gabriel is called the "angel of the Lord" or "an angel of the Lord" in Luke 1. Consequently, he is likely the one who appeared to Joseph a number of times as the angel of the Lord.

Other appearances of the angel of the Lord in the New Testament may be attributed to him. However, of this we cannot be certain.

Who Is The Angel Of The LORD In The Old Testament?

Though all the good angels are angels of God, or angels of the Lord, there is one special angel who is distinct and unique from all the other angels, he is called "the angel of the LORD" or "an angel of the Lord."

HE APPEARS IN BOTH TESTAMENTS

The Bible, in both testaments, speaks of this personage called "the angel of the LORD," the "angel of the Presence" or the "angel, or messenger, of the Covenant." He appears in many important contexts in Scripture. Indeed, the manner in which he is described sets him apart from all the other angels.

His appearances bring up a number of important questions. Who is he? Is he more than just a mere angel? What conclusions can we make about his identity from the Bible?

THERE ARE THREE POSSIBILITIES AS TO HIS IDENTITY

Three major views have been put forth as to the exact identity of the angel of the LORD. They are as follows.

Option 1: He was mighty angel who acted as the special representative of the LORD.

Option 2: He is God the Father assuming a human body.

Option 3: He is God the Son, taking a body for a short period of time.

Each of these three views has its supporters.

THE APPEARANCES OF THE ANGEL OF THE LORD

To determine which view best fits the evidence, we will consider some of the major appearances of the angel of the LORD and make some observations about those appearances.

1. HE APPEARED TO HAGAR

The first recorded appearance of the angel of the LORD was to Hagar, Abraham's mistress, and the mother of his son Ishmael. We read in Genesis.

> The angel added, "I will so increase your descendants that they will be too numerous to count" (Genesis 16:10 NIV).

This angel spoke in the first person to Hagar when he made her this promise. Indeed, he said that "He Himself" would multiply the descendants of Hagar. The angel therefore, identified Himself with the Lord.

After the appearance of the angel of the LORD, Hagar said.

> She gave this name to the LORD who spoke to her: "You are the God who sees me," for she said, "I have now seen the One who sees me" (Genesis 16:13 NIV).

Hagar believed that she had spoken directly to God. Therefore, she seemingly thought the angel was indeed the Lord Himself.

2. HE APPEARED TO ABRAHAM AND SARAH AT MAMRE

Three men appeared to Abraham and his wife Sarah at the plains of Mamre. They had come to inform Abraham and Sarah concerning two matters. First, the son that God had promised them would be born to Abraham and Sarah the next year. Second, the evil cities of Sodom and Gomorrah would be destroyed. One of the three visitors who gave them this information is specifically called the LORD.

> The LORD appeared to Abraham by the oaks of Mamre, as he sat at the entrance of his tent in the heat of the day (Genesis 18:1 NRSV).

One of these there personages is identified as the Lord Himself.

3. THE ANGEL APPEARED TO ABRAHAM ON MOUNT MORIAH

On another occasion, God told Abraham to bring his son Isaac to Mount Moriah to be offered as a sacrifice. Abraham obeyed and was about to take Isaac's life when God intervened. The angel of the LORD stopped Abraham saying.

> Do not lay a hand on the boy or do anything to him. For now I know that you fear God, since you have not withheld your only son from Me (Genesis 22:12 HCSB).

The angel told Abraham that he had not withheld Isaac from "himself." This seems to indicate that it was the Lord that was speaking.

He then called a second time to Abraham.

> The angel of the Lord called to Abraham from heaven a second time and said, "I swear by myself, declares the Lord, that because you have done this and have not withheld your son, your only son, I will surely bless you and make your descendants as numerous as the stars in the sky and as the sand on the seashore. Your descendants will take possession of the cities of their enemies, and through your offspring all nations on earth will be blessed, because you have obeyed me" (Genesis 22:15-18 NIV).

In this next instance the angel of the LORD, who called out to Abraham, seems to be the Yahweh, the LORD Himself, since He used the first person "I" in describing Himself.

4. HE APPEARED SEVERAL TIMES TO JACOB

This angel appeared a number of times to Jacob. We read in Genesis.

> Then the angel of God said to me in the dream, 'Jacob,' and I said, 'Here I am!' (Genesis 31:11 ESV).

In this instance, he is called the "angel of God." Jacob wrestled all night with this personage who finally disabled him. The next morning Jacob understood that it was God Himself whom he had wrestled.

> And Jacob called the name of the place Peniel: "For I have seen God face to face, and my life is preserved" (Genesis 32:30 NKJV).

At the end of his life, Jacob spoke of God, and the angel of the LORD, as identical.

> The Angel who has delivered me from all harm—may he bless these boys. May they be called by my name and the names of my fathers Abraham and Isaac, and may they increase greatly upon the earth (Genesis 48:16 NIV).

Again, we find this particular angel identified with "the Lord."

5. MOSES AND THE BURNING BUSH

The angel of the LORD appeared to Moses in the burning bush. We read the following in the Book of Exodus.

> There the angel of the LORD appeared to him in flames of fire from within a bush. Moses saw that though the bush was on fire it did not burn up (Exodus 3:2 NIV).

The angel explained who He was.

> Then he said, "I am the God of your father, the God of Abraham, the God of Isaac and the God of Jacob." At this,

Moses hid his face, because he was afraid to look at God (Exodus 3:6 NIV).

The martyr Stephen emphasized this special event.

Forty years later, an angel appeared to Moses from a burning bush in the desert near Mount Sinai. Moses was surprised by what he saw. He went closer to get a better look, and the Lord said, "I am the God who was worshiped by your ancestors, Abraham, Isaac, and Jacob." Moses started shaking all over and didn't dare to look at the bush (Acts 7:30-32 CEV).

This was a monumental event in the history of God's dealings with humanity. Scripture seems to indicate that it was the Lord Himself who appeared as an angel.

6. GOD'S PROMISE TO SEND HIS ANGEL

God promised to send His angel ahead of the children of Israel. In the Book of Exodus, we read the following promise of God.

See, I am sending an angel ahead of you to guard you along the way and to bring you to the place I have prepared. Pay attention to him and listen to what he says. Do not rebel against him; he will not forgive your rebellion, since my Name is in him. If you listen carefully to what he says and do all that I say, I will be an enemy to your enemies and will oppose those who oppose you. My angel will go ahead of you and bring you into the land of the Amorites, Hittites, Perizzites, Canaanites, Hivites and Jebusites, and I will wipe them out (Exodus 23:20-23 NIV).

The Israelites were told that they must obey this angel because the name of the LORD was in him. Since God would never share His name with any created being, it seems that this angel must be God Himself. Isaiah the prophet wrote.

I am Yahweh, that is My name; I will not give My glory to another or My praise to idols (Isaiah 42:8 HCSB).

The New Living Translation says.

I am the LORD; that is my name! I will not give my glory to anyone else. I will not share my praise with carved idols (Isaiah 42:8 NLT).

God specifically says that HE will not share His name or glory with anyone else. This is why many people think that this particular angel, this messenger, must be God Himself.

7. JOSHUA

An imposing personage appeared to Joshua. Scripture records the following.

Now when Joshua was near Jericho, he looked up and saw a man standing in front of him with a drawn sword in his hand. Joshua went up to him and asked, "Are you for us or for our enemies?" "Neither," he replied, "but as commander of the army of the LORD I have now come." Then Joshua fell facedown to the ground in reverence, and asked him, "What message does my Lord have for his servant?" The commander of the LORD's army replied, "Take off your sandals, for the place where you are standing is holy." And Joshua did so (Joshua 5:13-15 NIV).

Having Joshua immediately remove his sandals reminds one of the LORD telling Moses to remove his sandals in God's presence at the burning bush. This seems to be another indication that it was the Lord Himself who made an appearance to Joshua.

8. TO THE PEOPLE OF ISRAEL AT GILGAL

The angel of the Lord also appeared to the people of Israel. We read the following account.

Now the angel of the Lord went up from Gilgal to Bochim. And he said, "I brought you up from Egypt and brought you into the land that I swore to give to your fathers. I said, 'I will never break my covenant with you, and you shall make no covenant with the inhabitants of this land; you shall break down their altars.' But you have not obeyed my voice. What is this you have done? So now I say, I will not drive them out before you, but they shall become thorns in your sides, and their gods shall be a snare to you." As soon as the angel of the Lord spoke these words to all the people of Israel, the people lifted up their voices and wept. And they called the name of that place Bochim. And they sacrificed there to the Lord (Judges 2:1-5 NIV).

Notice this angel said that "I" have brought you up from Egypt. He spoke of the land that "I swore to give to your fathers." He also spoke about "my covenant" with you. These are references which can only refer to God and to Him alone. This is another example as to why many people believe the angel of the Lord was the Lord Himself.

9. GIDEON

Gideon was a man who was called by God to raise an army to defeat the innumerable Midianites. Because Gideon was a timid person, God paid him a visit to assure him that all would go well. After the encounter Gideon exclaimed.

Then Gideon perceived that he was the angel of the Lord. And Gideon said, "Alas, O Lord God! For now I have seen the angel of the Lord face to face." But the Lord said to him, "Peace be to you. Do not fear; you shall not die" (Judges 6:22,23 ESV).

If it was only an angel, and not God, that Gideon saw, then why was he afraid for his life?

10. SAMSON'S PARENTS

The angel of the LORD appeared to a Hebrew woman and her husband to announce the birth of a son, Samson. He was to deliver the people of Israel from their enemies.

> When the angel of the LORD did not show himself again to Manoah and his wife, Manoah realized that it was the angel of the LORD. "We are doomed to die!" he said to his wife. "We have seen God!" (Judges 13:21,22 NIV).

They identified the angel of the LORD with God Himself.

OTHER APPEARANCES WHERE HE IS DISTINGUISHED FROM THE LORD

Although these ten appearances identify the angel of the LORD with the LORD Himself, there are other appearances of the angel of the LORD where he is distinguished from God. We read the following in Second Samuel.

> So the Lord sent a pestilence on Israel from the morning until the appointed time. And there died of the people from Dan to Beersheba 70,000 men. And when the angel stretched out his hand toward Jerusalem to destroy it, the Lord relented from the calamity and said to the angel who was working destruction among the people, "It is enough; now stay your hand." And the angel of the Lord was by the threshing floor of Araunah the Jebusite (2 Samuel 24:15-16 ESV).

In this instance, the Lord stopped the destruction that the "angel of the Lord" was causing to Israel.

Zechariah wrote the following.

> And they reported to the angel of the LORD, who was standing among the myrtle trees, "We have gone throughout the earth and found the whole world at rest and in peace."

Then the angel of the LORD said, "LORD Almighty, how long will you withhold mercy from Jerusalem and from the towns of Judah, which you have been angry with these seventy years?" So the LORD spoke kind and comforting words to the angel who talked with me (Zechariah 1:11-13 NIV).

In this particular episode, the angel of the Lord is in a dialogue with the Lord Himself. The fact that this angel is asking questions, so as to gather information, reveals that He cannot be identified with God, the One who knows all things.

In these two instances, the angel of the Lord is differentiated from the Lord Himself.

THE ANGEL CAME AT TURNING POINTS IN HISTORY

One of the amazing things we discover about the "angel of the Lord" is how often this personage appeared at a turning point in history.

For example, this angel appeared to Abraham and Sarah to announce the son of promise was to be born. From their son Isaac, the chosen race would emerge.

The angel also spoke to Moses at the burning bush declaring that he would be the one who would deliver this same chosen people from the bondage of Egypt

The angel of the Lord also led the people of Israel to Mt. Sinai where the Law was given.

It was the angel of the Lord who ordered that an altar should be built on the threshing floor of the Araunah the Jebusite. This location would later become the place where the temple was built.

In sum, the angel of Lord appeared at a number of crucial times in the history of the people of God.

SUMMARY TO QUESTION 24
WHO IS THE ANGEL OF THE LORD IN THE OLD TESTAMENT?

While the Bible records angels visiting the people of God during the Old Testament era, there is one special angel who had a unique ministry. This personage is called the "angel of the Lord."

On ten separate occasions, when this particular angel appeared, he spoke as though it was the Lord Himself that was doing the talking. This includes appearances to such biblical characters as Abraham, Jacob, Moses, Joshua and Gideon.

Since we find this particular angel speaking in the same way that God Himself would speak, it has generated much discussion as to his exact identity. We will examine the issue of his identity in our next two questions.

QUESTION 25

Was The Angel Of The Lord In The Old Testament A Theophany? (A Temporary ppearance Of God)

We have seen that the angel of the Lord appeared at numerous times in the history of Israel during the Old Testament era. Furthermore, on ten of these occasions when He appeared, this angel spoke in the same way that God Himself would speak. This has caused many people to believe that the angel of the Lord was actually God Himself, taking upon a human form for a short period of time. This temporary appearance of God in a human form is known as a "theophany."

Is this what we should conclude? Did God Himself appear as the angel of the Lord at certain times during the Old Testament period?

The case for the angel of the LORD being a theophany, a temporary appearance of God in a body, is as follows.

1. HE IS IDENTIFIED WITH THE LORD HIMSELF

In some contexts, the angel of the LORD is identified with the LORD (Genesis 16:7-13; 22:11-18). Indeed, He speaks in the first person as the Lord.

2. HE HAS POWER TO GIVE LIFE

The angel of the LORD is said to have power to give life. We read of this in the Book of Genesis when this personage is addressing Hagar.

The angel of the Lord also said to her, "I will surely multiply your offspring so that they cannot be numbered for multitude" (Genesis 16:10 ESV).

Only God has this power. No angel or any other created being can do this.

3. HE IS ALL-KNOWING

The quality of omniscience, or knowing everything, is attributed to the angel of the LORD

> She gave this name to the Lord who spoke to her: "You are the God who sees me," for she said, "I have now seen the One who sees me" (Genesis 16:13 NIV).

Again we emphasize, the knowledge of angels is limited.

4. HE IS THE JUDGE OF THE EARTH

The angel of the LORD is called the "Judge of all the earth" (Genesis 18:25). This is a title that belongs to God alone. Angels do not judge the entire earth.

5. HE CAN FORGIVE SIN

The Bible says that only God can forgive sin. We read the Lord saying in Isaiah.

> "It is I who sweep away your transgressions for My own sake and remember your sins no more" (Isaiah 43:25 HCSB).

Yet the angel of the LORD had authority to forgive sins. The Lord said the following to the people of Israel.

> See, I am sending an angel ahead of you to guard you along the way and to bring you to the place I have prepared. Pay attention to him and listen to what he says. Do not rebel

against him; he will not forgive your rebellion, since my Name is in him (Exodus 23:20,21 NIV).

This equates the angel with the Lord Himself.

6. HE RECEIVES WORSHIP

Worship belongs to God and Him alone. Yet we are told that Moses and Joshua worshiped the angel of the LORD.

These facts have led many to believe that the angel of the Lord should be identified with the Lord Himself. In other words, on certain occasions in the Old Testament period, God Himself took on a human form in temporary appearances to His people.

In sum, we find that this particular angel is unique and distinct from all other angels mentioned in the Bible. Indeed, on occasion, he introduced himself as Deity, and yet he is distinct from God. While he spoke face to face with people as a man, the evidence seems clear that he was more than a simple messenger sent from God.

THE CASE FOR THE ANGEL OF THE LORD BEING GOD THE SON (JESUS CHRIST)

The evidence from these appearances has convinced many that, at certain times in the past, God took upon Himself a human form to appear to people as the angel of the LORD. This being the case we then must examine the evidence to see which member of the Trinity became the "angel of the Lord."

If the angel of the Lord was truly an appearance of God in human form, it seems that it is God the Son, the Second Person of the Trinity who made these appearances. Therefore, before He came to earth to live as a human being, the pre-incarnate Christ appeared to a number of people. The reasoning is as follows.

For one thing, the angel is called "Yahweh," the Lord. He is identified with God Himself. Therefore, the angel is the Lord Himself.

Although the angel is called "the Lord" He is sometimes treated as a distinct Person from the Lord. This is consistent with the doctrine of the Trinity where the three members are distinct from one another.

Therefore, if the angel is the Lord Himself, but is distinct from the other members of the Trinity, we then must identify which member He is. The best candidate is God the Son, Jesus Christ. The identification with God the Son, Jesus Christ, is made as follows.

1. ONLY GOD THE SON HAS ASSUMED A HUMAN BODY

In the New Testament, God the Father is unseen, as is God the Holy Spirit. While we hear the voice of the Father on a number of occasions, and the Holy Spirit comes down in the form of a dove, only God the Son took upon Himself a human body.

Therefore, it is consistent with what we know about God the Son, that He would appear in a human body on a few select occasions during the Old Testament period before He became a human being in the Person of Jesus Christ in the New Testament era.

2. THE NATURE OF THE MINISTRY OF THE ANGEL OF THE LORD IDENTIFIES HIM WITH GOD THE SON

When one looks at the ministry of the angel of the Lord, it is consistent with the ministry of God the Son. The angel of the Lord is sent to God's people to reveal His truth, while God the Son was sent to the world to reveal God's truth, as well as to reveal what God is like.

As the New Testament indicates that the Father sent the Son into the world, God the Father also sent the angel of the Lord into certain situations during the Old Testament period.

THE ANGEL OF THE LORD IS NOT IDENTIFIED WITH THE LORD IN THE NEW TESTAMENT

In the New Testament all reference to angels are to either human or angelic beings. Indeed, there is no instance where the angel of the Lord

QUESTION 25

is identified with the Lord Himself. This gives further indication that once God became a human being in the Person of Jesus Christ, it was no longer necessary for Him to appear to select people as an angel in a human form.

These arguments are used to show that the "angel of the Lord" and God the Son are one-in-the same Person.

SOMETIMES THE ANGEL OF THE LORD IS ACTUALLY GOD WHILE AT OTHER TIMES HE IS ONLY AN ANGEL

While the angel of the LORD is sometimes identified with the LORD Himself, there are other times when they are distinguished. Therefore, it is concluded that on some occasions the angel of the LORD was God Himself, while at other times he was merely a messenger sent from the LORD.

The context must determine the identity of the angel of the LORD. If the angel of the LORD was, in some instances, God the Son, Jesus Christ, coming in a temporary body, then the term angel stresses the basic meaning of the word—one sent. God the Son was sent by God the Father. Therefore the word "angel" in that context would be referring to the office of the One sent—a messenger.

This is in keeping with nature of the mission of Jesus Christ—He is the one whom the Father has sent. Jesus Himself said.

I am one who testifies for myself; my other witness is the Father, who sent me (John 8:18 NIV).

If, however, it is one of the angelic host who is referred to as the angel of the LORD, then it is the nature of the being that is being stressed. In other words, he is one of the heavenly host, a created spirit-being, who was sent from the Lord.

This sums up some of the arguments for the angel of the Lord being a theophany.

171

SUMMARY TO QUESTION 25
WAS THE ANGEL OF THE LORD IN THE OLD TESTAMENT A THEOPHANY? (A TEMPORARY APPEARANCE OF GOD)

As we have observed, on a number of occasions in the Old Testament, an angelic messenger appeared to select individuals as the "angel of the Lord." There is a question as to his exact identity.

Indeed, this personage spoke as if he were God Himself, and did things that only the Lord can do. In addition, on a few occasions he seemed to have been worshipped, something which belongs to God alone.

When the angel of the Lord appeared, it seems to be the Lord Himself. The angel has attributes that belong to God and God alone. In addition, He is addressed as the Lord, and he speaks in the first person as though He is the Lord. If this be the case, then He is not a created being, but God Himself who took on angelic form.

Though some have thought it to be God the Father, this would more likely be an instance of God the Son, the Second Person of the Trinity, coming to earth for a short time in a human form.

Other times, however, the angel of the Lord is clearly distinguished from the Lord. On these occasions the angel may have been a created being rather than God Himself.

This has led some to argue that the designation "angel of the Lord" may not always refer to Lord taking on a human form. It all depends upon the context.

QUESTION 26

Was The Angel Of The Lord Merely A Mighty Angel Who Was God's Special Representative?

While the idea that the angel of the Lord is a theophany, or Christophany, a temporary appearance of God the Son in a human form for the benefit of the people, there are those who believe that each appearance can better be explained by assuming that it was merely a mighty angel who appeared. The reasons why this position is held can be summarized as follows.

THE UNDERSTANDING OF THE ROLE OF A MESSENGER IN THE ANCIENT WORLD

To begin with, it is acknowledged that the angel speaks in the first person for God and that characteristics which belong to God alone are also applied to him. In other words, it appears as though this is God Himself speaking. However, this should not settle the issue seeing that we must understand the nature of the role of a messenger in the ancient world.

The ancients viewed a messenger as one who had the authority to speak for the one who sent him. Consequently the messenger could speak in the first person as though the one who sent him was actually speaking.

Consequently, while the messenger could personally make certain statements and claims, it was understood by everyone that the claims he was making were not his, but rather the one who sent him.

If this is the case, then it would explain why the angel of the Lord makes these specific claims for himself. He is speaking with the authority of the One who sent Him, the Lord.

OBJECTIONS TO THE IDEA THE ANGEL WAS NOT THE LORD HIMSELF

There are certain objections to this idea that the angel of the Lord was not actually the Lord taking upon Himself a human form.

First, at certain times, these angels received worship, something which belongs to God alone. This would disqualify a mere angel as being the angel of the Lord.

Second, it seems Hagar and the parents of Samson assumed they had actually seen the Lord Himself. Does this not prove that it was the Lord who in fact appeared?

RESPONSE TO OBJECTION: IT IS NOT CLEAR THE ANGELS RECEIVED WORSHIP

One of the strongest arguments for identifying the angel of the Lord with the Lord Himself is that he received worship; something that God alone is due. However, it is also been contended that this angel did not actually receive worship that belongs only to the Lord.

RESPONSE TO OBJECTION: WE SHOULD NOT ASSUME THAT HAGAR WAS CORRECT

While it seems that Hagar and the parents of Samson may have believed that the personage who spoke to them was God Himself this does not necessarily make it so. What we have recorded in Scripture is their belief in the identity of the personage which they saw.

Though these people believed they actually saw God this does not make it so. They could have been mistaken in their belief.

THE ANGEL OF THE LORD IN THE NEW TESTAMENT IS NOT GOD

There is something else. The angel of the Lord also appears in the New Testament. All agree that this personage is merely a messenger of God, a created being, and not God Himself.

CONCLUSION: THERE IS NO CLEAR SOLUTION TO THIS ISSUE

With the available evidence, it is possible to argue for either of these two choices. It is possible that the angel of the Lord, in some instances, was the pre-incarnate Christ, while it is also possible to believe that he is merely a special angel sent by God. The emphasis in Scripture is not so much on the messenger himself, but rather the message that he brought.

SUMMARY TO QUESTION 26
WAS THE ANGEL OF THE LORD MERELY A MIGHTY ANGEL WHO WAS GOD'S SPECIAL REPRESENTATIVE?

On a number of occasions in the Old Testament, an angelic messenger appeared to select individuals as the "angel of the Lord." There is a question as to his exact identity. This personage spoke as if he were God Himself, and did things that only the Lord can do. In addition, on a few occasions he seemed to have been worshipped, something which belongs to God alone.

When the angel of the Lord appeared, it seems to have been the Lord Himself. This angel has attributes that belong to God and to Him alone. In addition, He is addressed as the Lord, and He speaks in the first person as though He is the Lord. If this be the case, then He is not a created being, but God Himself who took on the role of a messenger.

Though some have thought it to be God the Father, this would more likely be an instance of God the Son, the Second Person of the Trinity, coming to earth for a short time in a human form.

Other times, however, the angel of the Lord is clearly distinguished from the Lord. On these occasions the angel may have been a created being rather than God Himself. This has led some to argue that the designation "angel of the Lord" may not always refer to Lord taking on a human form. It all depends upon the context.

However, we do not necessarily have to assume that it was the Lord Himself who appeared in a temporary form during Old Testament times. During the Old Testament period it was assumed that a messenger could speak with the absolute authority of the one who sent him.

Although the messenger would speak in the first person "I," everyone understood that it was the one who sent the messenger who was really speaking. If this is the case with the appearances of the angel of the Lord, then what we have is a heavenly messenger, not the Lord Himself, speaking to the people with the Lord's authority. The fact that this messenger uses the first person "I" does not necessarily mean that this messenger was the Lord.

There does not seem to be enough information to know which of these views is correct. It is possible that God Himself, in the Person of God the Son, took on a human form for certain select occasions and appeared as the "angel of the Lord."

It is also possible that it was merely an angel who appeared as God's representative in these instances. This angel spoke with God's complete authority.

The Scripture itself does not seem to be so concerned about the identity of the "angel of the Lord" as it is with the message he proclaimed. This should also be our emphasis.

QUESTION 27

Who Is The Angel Of The LORD
In The New Testament?

On a few occasions in the Old Testament period, a being called "the angel of the Lord," or "an angel of the Lord," appeared to select individuals. Who was he?

Some argue that this personage was God the Son, Jesus Christ, who temporarily assumed a human form before He became a human being some two thousand years ago. Others, however, see this person as merely an angel who was representing the Lord. There is no unanimity of opinion among Bible-believers on this matter.

The Bible also says the angel of the LORD appeared in New Testament times. Do we know his identity? Is it the same angel who appeared at various times during the Old Testament period?

"AN" ANGEL OR "THE" ANGEL?

To begin with, there is one matter that needs to be addressed concerning the identity of the angel of the Lord in the New Testament. In the Greek text, there is no article before the words, "angel of the Lord." Therefore, it can be translated either "an angel of the Lord" or "the angel of the Lord." While a few English translations use the article "the" before the "angel of the Lord," the great majority do not.

From the New Testament, we discover the following things about this angel.

1. HE FORETOLD THE BIRTH OF JESUS

An angel of the Lord appeared to Joseph and foretold the birth of Jesus. This is recorded in Matthew's gospel. It says.

> But just when he had resolved to do this, an angel of the Lord appeared to him in a dream and said, "Joseph, son of David, do not be afraid to take Mary as your wife, for the child conceived in her is from the Holy Spirit. She will bear a son, and you are to name him Jesus, for he will save his people from their sins" (Matthew 1:20,21 NRSV).

In this context the angel is not identified.

2. GABRIEL IS CALLED AN ANGEL OF THE LORD

Luke, however, seemingly identifies this angel of the LORD as Gabriel. He writes.

> An angel of the Lord appeared to him, standing to the right of the altar of incense (Luke 1:11 HCSB).

Luke also wrote.

> The angel answered him, "I am Gabriel, who stands in the presence of God, and I was sent to speak to you and tell you this good news" (Luke 1:19 HCSB).

The angel Gabriel appeared to Elizabeth to Mary also.

> In the sixth month of Elizabeth's pregnancy, God sent the angel Gabriel to Nazareth, a town in Galilee, to a virgin pledged to be married to a man named Joseph, a descendant of David. The virgin's name was Mary. The angel went to her and said, "Greetings, you who are highly favored! The Lord is with you" (Luke 1:26-28 NIV).

Since Gabriel who appeared to Mary was earlier identified as "an angel of the Lord" to foretell the birth of John the Baptist, it seems to follow that the unnamed angel of the Lord who appeared to Joseph was also Gabriel. However, we cannot be certain of this because he is not named in his appearance to Joseph.

3. HE APPEARED AFTER THE BIRTH OF CHRIST

This particular angel of the Lord also appeared to Joseph after Jesus had been born. He warned Joseph that Herod was about to kill the child.

> After they were gone, an angel of the Lord suddenly appeared to Joseph in a dream, saying, "Get up! Take the child and His mother, flee to Egypt, and stay there until I tell you. For Herod is about to search for the child to destroy Him" (Matthew 2:13 HCSB).

He also spoke to Joseph after Herod had died. The angel told him that his family could return from Egypt.

> After Herod died, an angel of the Lord suddenly appeared in a dream to Joseph in Egypt, saying, "Get up! Take the child and His mother and go to the land of Israel, because those who sought the child's life are dead (Matthew 2:19,20 HCSB).

Since Jesus had already been born, it is not possible that He could be both the young child, and this angel of the LORD, at the same time. Therefore this angel, or messenger, of the LORD in this context, was someone else.

4. HE DELIVERED PETER

An angel of the Lord helped Peter escape from jail. This is recorded in the Book of Acts.

> Suddenly an angel of the Lord appeared and a light shone in the cell. He tapped Peter on the side and woke him, saying, "Get up quickly." And the chains fell off his wrists (Acts 12:7 NRSV).

God used this angel of the Lord to keep Peter from being harmed by the religious rulers. Scripture says this angel of the Lord "appeared" in Peter's cell.

As spirit-beings, angels can function as go-betweens, between the Lord and humans. Indeed, they can pass back and forth from the unseen realm to the visible realm at will. In other words, these ministering spirits are unimpeded by any physical boundaries.

5. AN ANGEL OF THE LORD KILLED HEROD

An angel of the LORD is the one who put the evil king Herod to death. We read about this in the Book of Acts.

> Herod came dressed in his royal robes. He sat down on his throne and made a speech. The people shouted, "You speak more like a god than a man!" At once an angel from the Lord struck him down because he took the honor that belonged to God. Later, Herod was eaten by worms and died (Acts 12:21-23 CEV).

Though the angel of the LORD is not identified in these instances, there is nothing to suggest that he was the LORD Himself.

In these two instances, this angel of the Lord could not have been the Lord Jesus. Indeed, these two episodes occurred after His ascension into heaven. Once the Lord had come back from the dead, He always appeared as the "resurrected Christ," never as an angel.

IT IS PROBABLY GABRIEL

The most likely candidate for the angel of the Lord in the New Testament is Gabriel. As we mentioned, when an angel of the Lord appeared to Zechariah to announce the birth of John the Baptist, he identified himself as Gabriel.

Though we are not specifically told the identity of this angel of the Lord in the other New Testament contexts, it is consistent to identify him with the angel Gabriel. However, we cannot be certain.

SUMMARY TO QUESTION 27
WHO IS THE ANGEL OF THE LORD IN THE NEW TESTAMENT?

There is no agreement as to the exact identity of a personage called "the angel of the Lord" or "an angel of the Lord" in the New Testament. Some believe it was actually God the Son, Jesus Christ, who appeared as the angel of the Lord during certain times in the Old Testament era. Others contend it was merely a messenger of God who was the angel of the Lord, and not God Himself taking on a human form.

While the angel of the Lord may have been God the Son, Jesus Christ, making temporary appearances on certain occasions in the Old Testament, it certainly was not the same person appearing during the New Testament era.

The angel Gabriel is identified as "the angel of the Lord" by Luke. Gabriel appeared to Zechariah the father of John the Baptist announcing the upcoming birth of John. This occurred before the birth of Christ.

An angel of the Lord foretold the birth of Jesus to Joseph. However, on two other occasions when the angel of the Lord appeared to Joseph, Jesus had already been born.

Obviously the angel of the Lord could not have been Jesus! This tells us that the phrase "angel of the Lord" either speaks of more than one person, or that the same person was involved in all the appearances under the title "angel of the Lord."

There are two other recorded appearances in the New Testament of the angel of the Lord. They both occur in the Book of Acts. The angel of the Lord miraculously delivered Peter from prison before he was to be brought before the religious rulers.

Later, the angel of the Lord struck down the evil King Herod when Herod glorified himself rather than giving glory to God. Since these appearances took place after Jesus had ascended into heaven, it rules out Him being the angel of the Lord in these instances. Whenever Jesus appeared after His resurrection, He is identified as the resurrected Christ.

If the angel of the Lord does not refer to Jesus during these New Testament appearances, then possibly it would not have been the Lord Jesus in those Old Testament appearances as the "angel of the Lord."

Since Gabriel is identified as the angel of the Lord in Luke, we should probably assume that it is he who appears in other contexts in the New Testament, but is not named.

QUESTION 28

Are Angels Connected With The Various Nations?

We find from Scripture that there is a connection between angels and the different nations of the world. When the Jews were about to return from captivity, the prophet Daniel began to pray and fast for their coming back. At this time the Jews were under the rule of the Persian Empire. After three weeks of prayer, an angel appeared and explained to Daniel the reason for the delay. The Book of Daniel explained why it happened in this manner.

> Only I, Daniel, saw the vision; the men who were with me did not see it. On the contrary, they were overcome with fright and ran away to hide. I alone was left to see this great vision. My strength drained from me, and my vigor disappeared; I was without energy. I listened to his voice and as I did so I fell into a trance-like sleep with my face to the ground. Then a hand touched me and set me on my hands and knees. He said to me, "Daniel, you are of great value. Understand the words that I am about to speak to you. So stand up, for I have now been sent to you." When he said this to me, I stood up shaking. Then he said to me, "Don't be afraid, Daniel, for from the very first day you applied your mind to understand and to humble yourself before your God, your words were heard. I have come in response to your words. However, the prince of the kingdom of Persia

was opposing me for twenty-one days. But Michael, one of the leading princes, came to help me, because I was left there with the kings of Persia. Now I have come to help you understand what will happen to your people in the latter days, for the vision pertains to future days" (Daniel 10:7-14 NET).

This passage gives us some insight into the battles occurring in the spiritual realm. We can make the following observations from this passage.

1. THERE IS A SPIRITUAL BATTLE OCCURRING

It took this angel twenty-one days to answer Daniel's prayer because the prince of the kingdom of Persia hindered him. Obviously this could not have been an earthly prince restraining an angel. Therefore, this passage speaks of a spiritual battle that is occurring in the heavenly realm.

In the New Testament, we find this emphasized.

> For our battle is not against flesh and blood, but against the rulers, against the authorities, against the world powers of this darkness, against the spiritual forces of evil in the heavens (Ephesians 6:12 HCSB).

There is indeed a spiritual battle.

2. THE PRINCE OF PERSIA IS OVERSEEING THE NATION

The prince of Persia seems to be the angel that was overseeing this nation. For some reason he was opposed to revealing this message to Daniel about what would occur in the future. Though no specific details are given, we are informed by this passage that there was an angel overseeing Persia in the same way as the Lord used Michael as the overseer of the nation Israel.

3. THERE IS ALSO THE PRINCE OF GREECE

From this passage we are informed that there is also a prince, or angel, over Greece. We read the following.

So he said, "Do you know why I have come to you? Soon I will return to fight against the prince of Persia, and when I go, the prince of Greece will come" (Daniel 10:20 NIV).

After his battle with the prince of Persia, this angel said the angel, or prince, of Greece was to come. This angel that looked after Greece, like the one over Persia, was not inclined to allow Daniel to be informed of events which were to come.

4. ANGELS ARE DESCRIBED AS RULERS IN THE NEW TESTAMENT

When the New Testament uses the word "rulers" to describe the different orders or ranks of angels, this may include these various angels over the nations. The word is used of both good and bad angels. Paul wrote.

So that through the church the wisdom of God in its rich variety might now be made known to the rulers and authorities in the heavenly places (Ephesians 3:10 NRSV).

He said that our ultimate struggle is against these authorities.

For our struggle is not against enemies of blood and flesh, but against the rulers, against the authorities, against the cosmic powers of this present darkness, against the spiritual forces of evil in the heavenly places (Ephesians 6:12 NRSV).

Ultimately, the struggle that believers face is with these spiritual powers in the heavenly realm.

In sum, the Lord has pulled back the curtain of the unseen realm to let us know that there are spiritual battles among angels who are aligned with various nations. While this gives us a glimpse into the unseen realm, there is obviously so much that we do not know. Therefore, we must be careful not to speculate beyond what has been revealed.

SUMMARY TO QUESTION 28
ARE ANGELS CONNECTED WITH THE VARIOUS NATIONS?

From Scripture there seems to be angels which actually oversee the various nations. The prayer of Daniel the prophet gives examples of angels looking over the affairs of Greece and Persia.

Daniel was told by an angel that the answer to his prayers was hindered for three weeks by the prince of Persia. Michael the archangel had to assist another angel in bringing Daniel the answer to his request. Obviously there was spiritual warfare occurring in the heavenly realm which prevented his prayers from being answered.

This certainly tells us that there are spiritual battles occurring in heavenly places. This is consistent with what Paul wrote to the Ephesians. Indeed, our struggle is ultimately with spiritual forces, not with humans.

In addition, this passage seems to indicate that there are certain angels who have authority over nations. As Michael the archangel is said to be the guardian of Israel, this angel of Persia was guiding this evil nation. This angel over Persia did not want Daniel to be informed about future events; events which would deal directly with that nation.

An angel over Greece is also mentioned. This particular angel did not want Daniel to understand what would happen to that nation in the future.

From these passages we are again reminded that ultimately we are fighting spiritual battles against unseen spiritual forces. These forces are powerful and evil but they have been defeated by the Lord. In this, we can take much comfort.

QUESTION 29

Who Are The Living Creatures? (Ezekiel 1, Revelation 4)

While the subject of this book is angels, God's invisible messengers, there are other heavenly beings that the Lord has created that are always kept distinct from the angels. In other words, these beings are never sent as God's emissaries to humanity as are the angels.

The Book of Ezekiel describes certain heavenly beings called "living creatures." Their description is found in the opening chapter. It reads as follows.

> And in the fire was what looked like four living creatures. In appearance their form was that of a man, but each of them had four faces and four wings. Their legs were straight; their feet were like those of a calf and gleamed like burnished bronze. Under their wings on their four sides they had the hands of a man. All four of them had faces and wings, and their wings touched one another. Each one went straight ahead; they did not turn as they moved. Their faces looked like this: Each of the four had the face of a man, and on the right side each had the face of a lion, and on the left the face of an ox; each also had the face of an eagle. Such were their faces. Their wings were spread out upward; each had two wings, one touching the wing of another creature on either side, and two wings covering its body. Each one went

straight ahead. Wherever the spirit would go, they would go, without turning as they went (Ezekiel 1:5-12 NIV).

The description Ezekiel gives of these creatures is both complicated and puzzling—they are merely called "four living creatures" and nothing more. In this context, we have no other clue to their identity.

SOME THINK THEY ARE THE CHERUBIM

Though the living creatures are not identified in Ezekiel 1, we may have an explanation of their identity later in Ezekiel. In another vision, Ezekiel sees heavenly creatures that he calls, "cherubim."

The cherubim were standing at the south end of the Temple when the man went in, and the cloud of glory filled the inner courtyard. Then the glory of the LORD rose up from above the cherubim and went over to the door of the Temple. The Temple was filled with this cloud of glory, and the Temple courtyard glowed brightly with the glory of the LORD. The moving wings of the cherubim sounded like the voice of God Almighty and could be heard clearly in the outer courtyard. The LORD said to the man in linen clothing, "Go between the cherubim and take some burning coals from between the wheels." So the man went in and stood beside one of the wheels. Then one of the cherubim reached out his hand and took some live coals from the fire burning among them. He put the coals into the hands of the man in linen clothing, and the man took them and went out. (All the cherubim had what looked like human hands hidden beneath their wings.) Each of the four cherubim had a wheel beside him, and the wheels sparkled like chrysolite. All four wheels looked the same; each wheel had a second wheel turning crosswise within it. The cherubim could move forward in any of the four directions they faced, without turning as they moved. They went straight in the direction in which their heads were turned, never turning aside. Both the cherubim and the wheels were covered with eyes. The cherubim had eyes all over their bodies, including their hands, their backs, and their wings. I heard someone refer to the wheels as "the whirling wheels." Each of the four cherubim had four faces—the first was the face of an ox, the second was a human face, the third was the face of a lion, and the fourth was the face of an eagle (Ezekiel 10:3-14 NLT).

Because this description is similar to chapter 1, many people think they are two different descriptions of the same creatures—the cherubim.

REVELATION 4 SPEAKS OF LIVING CREATURES

Some identify them with the four living creatures spoken of in the Book of Revelation. The Bible says.

The first living creature like a lion, the second living creature like an ox, the third living creature with a face like a human face, and the fourth living creature like a flying eagle (Revelation 4:7 NRSV).

They had four faces: of a man, an ox, a lion, and an eagle. They seem to be representative of various parts of God's creation (humanity, domesticated animals, the wild beasts, and birds).

These living creatures worship God continually. The Bible tells us more about them.

Each of these living beings had six wings, and their wings were covered with eyes, inside and out. Day after day and night after night they keep on saying, "Holy, holy, holy is the Lord God Almighty— the one who always was, who is, and who is still to come" (Revelation 4:8 NLT).

Their mission is to constantly serve the living God.

THERE IS NOT ENOUGH INFORMATION TO BE CERTAIN

Though these beings are similar to the ones spoken of in Ezekiel, there are some differences between them. Whether they are the same creatures with slightly different descriptions, or two similar types of heavenly creatures, we cannot be certain. There is simply not enough information.

In sum, since there are so many things that we do not know about these living creatures, we must be extremely careful about making any firm conclusions.

SUMMARY TO QUESTION 29
WHO ARE THE LIVING CREATURES? (EZEKIEL 1, REVELATION 4)

In the first chapter of the writings of the prophet Ezekiel, he saw in a vision, four living creatures that were around the throne of God. Their identity is not explained.

In chapter 10 he gives a description of the cherubim—which could be the same creatures. However, no connection is made between the two passages.

We also find similar living creatures in the Book of Revelation. Though their characteristics are similar, they are not exactly the same.

Consequently we do not have enough information to make any definite conclusions about these heavenly creatures. The best we can say is that these creatures do exist and they have some function in God's rule but beyond that we must remain silent.

Who Are
The Cherubim?

Scripture speaks of heavenly beings known as cherubim. As is true with the "living creatures," they are distinct from the angels. In fact, the cherubim are seemingly the highest form of created beings.

The word "cherubim" is the plural form of "cherub." It is a transliteration of a Hebrew word. In other words, the Hebrew word here is cherubim and the English translators have merely transliterated it into English.

In some of the older English versions, "cherubim" was made plural by, "cherubims." This however, is a mistaken translation since cherubim is the plural form, and cherub the singular in Hebrew.

THE CHERUBIM IN SCRIPTURE

We find the cherubim mentioned a number of times in Scripture. They are as follows.

1. THE WERE GUARDING EDEN

Cherubim guarded the Garden of Eden after Adam and Eve were banished. The Book of Genesis reports what occurred.

> After he drove the man out, he placed on the east side
> of the Garden of Eden cherubim and a flaming sword

flashing back and forth to guard the way to the tree of life (Genesis 3:24 NIV).

They were placed there to keep Adam and Eve from re-entering the Garden and eating from the tree of life.

2. THE CHERUBIM WERE ON THE ATONEMENT COVER (THE MERCY SEAT)

The Bible describes two golden figures of the cherubim with their wings stretched over the Atonement Cover, or Mercy Seat, on the Ark of the Covenant. We read the following.

> And make two cherubim out of hammered gold at the ends of the cover. Make one cherub on one end and the second cherub on the other; make the cherubim of one piece with the cover, at the two ends. The cherubim are to have their wings spread upward, overshadowing the cover with them. The cherubim are to face each other, looking toward the cover. Place the cover on top of the ark and put in the ark the Testimony, which I will give you (Exodus 25:18-21 NIV).

God promised to meet with His people there. Scripture says.

> There, above the cover between the two cherubim that are over the ark of the Testimony, I will meet with you and give you all my commands for the Israelites (Exodus 25:22 NIV).

The cherubim were on this holy object, the place of meeting between God and His people.

3. THEIR FIGURE WAS ON THE VEIL OF TABERNACLE

The figure of the cherubim was interwoven into the veil of the tabernacle. The Bible says.

> Moreover you shall make the tabernacle with ten curtains of fine twisted linen, and blue, purple, and crimson yarns; you

shall make them with cherubim skillfully worked into them (Exodus 26:1 NRSV).

The importance of the cherubim can be found by their placement on the curtains of the tent of meeting, the tabernacle.

4. THERE WERE TWO CARVED CHERUBIM NEXT TO THE ARK

Two large-sized olivewood cherubim were constructed and placed next to the Ark of the Covenant in the Temple.

> Within the inner sanctuary Solomon placed two cherubim made of olive wood, each 15 feet tall. The wingspan of each of the cherubim was 15 feet, each wing being 7-1/2 feet long. The two cherubim were identical in shape and size; each was 15 feet tall. Solomon placed them side by side in the inner sanctuary of the Temple. Their outspread wings reached from wall to wall, while their inner wings touched at the center of the room (1 Kings 6:23-27 NLT).

These gigantic cherubim would have been imposing figures in the Holy of Holies.

5. THE LORD RODE A CHERUB

Scripture speaks of the Lord symbolically riding a cherub. The Bible says of Him.

> He rode on a cherub and flew, soaring on the wings of the wind (2 Samuel 22:11 HCSB).

The Bible also speaks of God as enthroned on the cherubim (Ezekiel 10:1-22).

WHO ARE THE CHERUBIM?

The cherubim are similar to the seraphim, but a different order of heavenly being. Their exact identity has not been revealed in Scripture. There are three main theories as to what they represent.

1. THEY ARE CONNECTED TO GOD'S JUDGMENT AND REDEMPTION

In some instances they seem to be connected to God's judgment and redemption of humanity (Genesis 3:24, Exodus 25:22).

2. THEY ARE SYMBOLIC REPRESENTATIVES OF THE GODHEAD

There are some who hold that the cherubim are symbolic representative of the Trinity—God the Father, God the Son, and God the Holy Spirit.

3. THEY ARE SYMBOLIC REPRESENTATIONS OF REDEEMED HUMANITY

Others contend that cherubim are actually symbolic of redeemed humanity. According to this view, the perfections of humanity that were lost at the fall in the Garden of Eden are now reflected in the cherubim. They represent, not fallen humanity, but redeemed humanity—they are symbolic of what God has done for us. Consequently they are placed near the symbolic presence of God.

THEY ARE SYMBOLS OF GOD'S MERCY

It seems what we can say is that the cherubim were symbols of the mercy of God. While the flaming sword in the Garden of Eden symbolized God's justice, the position of the cherubim, to keep them from re-entering the Garden, was a sign of God's mercy. The position of the cherubim over the Ark of the Covenant, and in the Holy of Holies, would also seem to speak of the mercy of God.

THEY ARE NEAR TO GOD

In addition, their nearness to God gives to all creation the assurance that someday it will be set free from the bondage of sin. The Bible says.

> For all creation is waiting eagerly for that future day when God
> will reveal who his children really are (Romans 8:19 NLT).

This is the day in which all redeemed humanity is looking forward to!

WHAT DID THEY LOOK LIKE?

Not only is the exact identity of the cherubim unknown, it is also not known how they looked. Some identify them with the living creatures of Ezekiel 1 and Revelation 4. If that is the case, then they would have four faces.

> The first living creature like a lion, the second living creature like an ox, the third living creature with the face of a man, and the fourth living creature like an eagle in flight (Revelation 4:7 ESV).

These four faces are thought to illustrate the strength of God's creatures; lion-like strength, ox-like service, human-like intelligence, and eagle-like speed.

Others, however, believe the cherubim had human faces and are not to be identified with the "living creatures" that had four faces.

In sum, while there are certain things we do know about the cherubim there is certainly much mystery with respect to exactly who they are, what they look like, as well as what they do.

SUMMARY TO QUESTION 30
WHO ARE THE CHERUBIM?

The cherubim were winged creatures that appear in a number of places in Scripture. They are seemingly the highest form of heavenly beings that the Lord has created. The Bible always keeps them distinct from angels, who are sent by the Lord as ministering spirits.

Scripture says that cherubim guarded the Garden of Eden after Adam and Eve sinned. We find their form was fashioned on the Ark of the Covenant, and two large carved cherubim were placed in the temple.

As to their exact identity and appearance, no one knows. It is not certain that they are the living creatures identified in Ezekiel 1 or Revelation 4. Much about them still remains a mystery. Therefore, we must be careful about making any firm conclusions.

QUESTION 31

Who Are
The Seraphim?

In the Book of Isaiah, there are heavenly beings called "seraphs" or "seraphim." As we have found with the cherubim and the living creatures, the seraphim are a distinct type of a created being that is different from the angels.

Seraphim is the plural form of the word "seraph." Like the term "cherubim," seraph and seraphim are both transliterations of Hebrew words. In other words, the Hebrew words found here in Isaiah are "seraph" and "seraphim." The English translators have merely transliterated the Hebrew words into our language.

The Bible gives this description of them.

> In the year that King Uzziah died, I saw the Lord, high and exalted, seated on a throne; and the train of his robe filled the temple. Above him were seraphim, each with six wings: With two wings they covered their faces, with two they covered their feet, and with two they were flying. And they were calling to one another: "Holy, holy, holy is the Lord Almighty; the whole earth is full of his glory." At the sound of their voices the doorposts and thresholds shook and the temple was filled with smoke (Isaiah 6:1-4 NIV).

The Bible then describes the response of the prophet Isaiah when he saw this vision.

"Woe to me!" I cried. "I am ruined! For I am a man of unclean lips, and I live among a people of unclean lips, and my eyes have seen the King, the Lord Almighty." Then one of the seraphim flew to me with a live coal in his hand, which he had taken with tongs from the altar. With it he touched my mouth and said, "See, this has touched your lips; your guilt is taken away and your sin atoned for" (Isaiah 6:5-7 NIV).

This is the only scriptural reference to the seraphim.

The word means "the burning ones." In the context of Isaiah, the seraphim are connected with God's throne and His holiness. They are standing and serving before the throne, awaiting His commands.

THE DESCRIPTION GIVEN

This passages provides for us a specific description of the seraphim. They also have a different appearance than angels as well as the cherubim. Note that they have six wings, with two covering their faces and two covering their feet. This is highly instructive. Indeed, even the seraphim cannot be fully exposed in the presence of the Living God who is Holy, Holy, Holy!

THEY WERE THE AGENT IN ISAIAH PURIFICATION

The seraphim were engaged in the purification of the prophet Isaiah. We read the following words of the prophet.

"Woe to me!" I cried. "I am ruined! For I am a man of unclean lips, and I live among a people of unclean lips, and my eyes have seen the King, the LORD Almighty" . . . With it he touched my mouth and said, "See, this has touched your lips; your guilt is taken away and your sin atoned for" (Isaiah 6:5,7 NIV).

Isaiah the prophet was purified by the work of these angels.

What all that means is not explained. Like other heavenly personages, such as the living creatures (Ezekiel 1, Revelation 4) and the cherubim, there is much that we do not know about the seraphim.

THEY SEEM TO BE PART OF THE HEAVENLY ASSEMBLY

It is possible that the seraphim are part of a group called the heavenly assembly, or heavenly counsel. We read about them as follows.

> Micaiah continued, "Therefore hear the word of the Lord: I saw the Lord sitting on his throne with all the multitudes of heaven standing around him on his right and on his left. And the Lord said, 'Who will entice Ahab into attacking Ramoth Gilead and going to his death there?' "One suggested this, and another that. Finally, a spirit came forward, stood before the Lord and said, 'I will entice him. Therefore, we must be careful about making any firm conclusions about exactly who they are, and what they do" (1 Kings 22:19-21 NIV).

There are some who believe that the "spirit" in this context may refer to the seraphim. However, there is not enough evidence to be certain.

DID THE SERAPHIM HAVE THE AUTHORITY TO FORGIVE SIN?

One question that does come up about the seraphim concerns their ability to forgive sin. In their description in the Book of Isaiah we read that after Isaiah saw a vision of the Lord Himself a seraph flew to him and told him that he was forgiven of his sin.

> I said, "Too bad for me! I am destroyed, for my lips are contaminated by sin, and I live among people whose lips are contaminated by sin. My eyes have seen the king, the Lord who commands armies." But then one of the seraphs flew toward me. In his hand was a hot coal he had taken from the altar with tongs. He touched my mouth with it and said, "Look, this coal has touched your lips. Your evil is removed; your sin is forgiven" (Isaiah 6:5-7 NET).

Was this seraph able to confer forgiveness on Isaiah? The answer is both yes and no. Yes, this spirit-being was able to tell Isaiah that he had been forgiven. However, the seraph did this as a representative of the Lord. In other words, this creature was merely conveying a message from the Lord that the prophet had been forgiven. This is an important distinction. Created beings, including humans, do not have the ability to forgive the sins of a person, only God does this. However, God's representatives, in speaking for Him, can bring the message that sins have been forgiven and cleansing has occurred. This is what happened in this instance.

In fact, it is similar to the authority Jesus gave to His disciples after He had risen from the dead. We read the following in the Gospel of John.

> So Jesus said to them again, "Peace be with you. Just as the Father has sent me, I also send you." And after he said this, he breathed on them and said, "Receive the Holy Spirit. If you forgive anyone's sins, they are forgiven; if you retain anyone's sins, they are retained" (John 20:21-23 NET).

Believers have the authority to tell people their sins have been forgiven, or their sins have not been forgiven. This is based upon how the person views Jesus Christ. Those who trust Him as their Savior are forgiven. Christians can declare this truth to the unbeliever. On the other hand, Christians are also able to tell people that their sins will not be forgiven if they reject Christ. This authority has been given to believers by the Lord. However, the ability to forgive belongs to Him alone. His representatives merely convey this truth.

This is similar to this episode with the seraph in Isaiah. In the vision of Isaiah, the seraph, as a representative of the Lord, declared that Isaiah's guilt was removed. However, this being, in and of itself, had no authority to do so.

SUMMARY TO QUESTION 31
WHO ARE THE SERAPHIM?

The seraphim, or burning ones, are only mentioned in one passage in Isaiah. They are somehow connected with the throne of God. They do not appear in the form of men as do angels. Indeed, they seem to be a higher rank of heavenly beings than the angels. Like the cherubim, they are depicted as having wings.

As is the case of other heavenly beings, such as the living creatures in Ezekiel and Revelation, and the cherubim, there is much that we do not know about the seraphim.

QUESTION 32

Who Are The
Elect Angels?

Scripture speaks of certain angels as being "elect." We find them mentioned a number of times in the Bible. For example, Paul wrote to Timothy.

> In the presence of God and of Christ Jesus and of the elect angels, I warn you to keep these instructions without prejudice, doing nothing on the basis of partiality (1 Timothy 5:21 NRSV).

The elect angels are most likely those who stayed true to God during the original angelic rebellion. There may have been a period of time when they were under probation. The fact that they remained true to the Lord revealed their election.

Believers are said to be "elect" or "chosen" for obedience."

> Peter, an apostle of Jesus Christ, To the pilgrims of the Dispersion in Pontus, Galatia, Cappadocia, Asia, and Bithynia, elect according to the foreknowledge of God the Father, in sanctification of the Spirit, for obedience and sprinkling of the blood of Jesus Christ: Grace to you and peace be multiplied (1 Peter 1:1,2 NKJV).

Like these angels, these believers willingly chose to follow the Lord when given the option. In this sense they are also "elect."

WHAT DO WE KNOW ABOUT ELECT ANGELS?

The Bible says the following about the elect angels.

1. THEY ARE CONFIRMED IN THEIR GOODNESS

These angels, who did not stray from the Lord, have been confirmed in their goodness. They are constantly loyal to the Lord. This is a permanent quality of their character.

2. THEY RELATE DIFFERENTLY THAN HUMANS

Because the elect angels do not need any deliverance from sin, as do humans, they are related to Jesus Christ differently. He is not their intermediary, as He is with humanity. Jesus serves as an intermediary between believers and God the Father. He has no such ministry with the "elect angels."

3. THEY HAVE NO WILL TO CHOOSE EVIL

It seems that the elect angels, or holy angels, now have no will to choose evil. They made their choice when they did not follow the devil. This choice seems to be an eternal, irrevocable decision on their part. In other words, there will not be another angelic rebellion in the future.

4. THEY ARE IN CONTRAST TO THE EVIL ANGELS

The elect angels are in contrast to those who rebelled with the devil. Judgment and then punishment is awaiting them. Jesus explained it this way.

> Then He will also say to those on the left, 'Depart from Me, you who are cursed, into the eternal fire prepared for the Devil and his angels!' (Matthew 25:41 HCSB).

These evil angels are cursed for their sin. In other words, there is no hope for them.

These are the few things we are told about the "elect" or "chosen" angels.

SUMMARY TO QUESTION 32
WHO ARE THE ELECT ANGELS?

Certain angels in Scripture are called "elect" or "chosen." These are the ones who did not rebel against God in the beginning, but rather chose to stay with Him when the rebellion occurred.

Like believers, their election was revealed when they chose to follow the Lord rather than the devil. It seems that once they made their choice in the beginning not to rebel, they are forever obedient to the Lord.

QUESTION 33

Why Are Angels Called "Winds" In Some Translations Of Hebrews 1:7 And "Spirits" In Other Translations?

In the first chapter of the Book of Hebrews, where the writer emphasizes that Jesus is superior to the angels, there is a description of angels in verse seven. However, we find a difference in the way this verse is translated into English.

ANGELS ARE SPIRITS

In many translations, the verse is rendered something like the following.

> And he says of the angels, "He makes his angels spirits and his ministers a flame of fire" (Hebrews 1:7 NET).

> In speaking of the angels he says, "He makes his angels spirits, and his servants flames of fire" (Hebrews 1:7 NIV).

In these translations, like many others, the Bible says that the Lord makes his angels "spirits."

OTHER TRANSLATIONS SAY WINDS

However, the plural form of the Greek word *pneuma*, translated here as "spirits," can also mean "winds."

In fact, some English translations render the word in this manner in this verse in Hebrews. For example, we read.

> And about the angels He says: He makes His angels winds, and His servants a fiery flame (Hebrews 1:7 HCSB).

> Of the angels he says, "He makes his angels winds, and his ministers a flame of fire" (Hebrews 1:7 ESV).

Consequently, we find a difference concerning how English translations render this verse.

THE WRITER IS QUOTING PSALM 104:4

In this passage, the writer to the Hebrews is citing the Psalms where we read the following.

> He [the Lord] lays the beams of his chambers on the waters; he makes the clouds his chariot; he rides on the wings of the wind; he makes his messengers winds, his ministers a flaming fire (Psalm 104:3,4 ESV).

In these verses, it is speaking poetically of the literal wind. The Lord can make the angels like the wind, or like a flaming fire.

SO WHAT IS THE PROPER TRANSLATION?

Since we find some translations reading "winds," while other "spirits," do we know which of the two is correct? The truth of the matter is that either is possible, and either will work in the context.

ANGELS ARE LIKE THE WIND

As we have observed, angels are compared to the wind in Scripture. This could also be drawing attention to their spirit nature. Indeed, they are invisible spirits, servants of the Living God. This particular verse in Hebrews compares angels to both wind and fire.

208

Interestingly, wind and fire are also symbols of the Person and work of the Holy Spirit in the Old Testament.

Consequently, wind and fire are fitting designations of both the Holy Spirit and angels since they each serve God the Father. Of course, angels are inferior beings to the Spirit of God.

In fact, this is the argument of the writer to the Hebrews. Even though the angels are as speedy as wind, and as powerful as fire, they are inferior beings to God the Son, Jesus.

ANGELS ARE SPIRITS

Later, in the same chapter, the angels are called "spirits."

> But to which of the angels has he ever said, "Sit at my right hand until I make your enemies a footstool for your feet"? Are they not all ministering spirits, sent out to serve those a who will inherit salvation (Hebrews 1:13,14 NET).

While the same Greek word is used in this verse as in verse seven, there is unanimous agreement that "spirits" is the correct translation here.

In sum, either translation of this Greek word will work in the context in Hebrews 1:7. Indeed, angels are spirit-beings whose ministry is like the changing wind.

SUMMARY TO QUESTION 33
WHY ARE ANGELS CALLED WINDS IN SOME TRANSLATIONS OF HEBREWS 1:7 AND SPIRITS IN OTHER TRANSLATIONS?

In the Book of Hebrews, there is a difference in English translations in verse seven of chapter one. Some translations say the angels are "spirits" while others say they are "winds." Why is this so, and which is right?

As we noted, the Greek word used here, the plural form of the word "pneuma," can have either meaning depending upon the context. We know that angels are spirits, since verse fourteen in this same chapter emphasizes this. We also know that angels can be compared to the wind as they are in Psalm 104.

In contrast to God the Son, who never changes, angels do change. It all depends upon the way the Lord desires to use them to minister to His people. So angels can be called "spirits" as in verse fourteen of chapter one because they are spirit-beings doing His service. On the other hand, it is also correct to compare them to the wind, since their ministry changes according to the will of the Lord.

We conclude that either translation can fit the context.

QUESTION 34

Does The Book Of Zechariah Speak About Female Angels?

As we study the Scripture, we discover that when angels appear to humans, they always appear as a man, never as a child, or as a female. In other words, they are always in a male form and they are always clothed.

Though angels are sexless creatures, neither male or female, we find this to be consistent throughout the Bible.

ARE THERE FEMALE ANGELS?

However, there is a passage in the Book of Zechariah that has led some to conclude that angels have appeared in a female form in the Bible. We read the following.

> Then the angel who was speaking to me came forward and said to me, "Look up and see what is appearing." I asked, "What is it?" He replied, "It is a basket." And he added, "This is the iniquity of the people throughout the land." Then the cover of lead was raised, and there in the basket sat a woman! He said, "This is wickedness," and he pushed her back into the basket and pushed its lead cover down on it. Then I looked up—and there before me were two women, with the wind in their wings! They had wings like those of a stork, and they lifted up the basket between heaven and earth. "Where

are they taking the basket?" I asked the angel who was speaking to me. He replied, "To the country of Babylonia to build a house for it. When the house is ready, the basket will be set there in its place" (Zechariah 5:5-11 NIV).

In this passage, we are introduced to two unidentified women who are described as having great wings like those of a stork. We find that they transport a measuring basket which contained a woman called wickedness. These two winged-women, brought the basket, with the woman, to the country of Babylonia. Recall, that the Book of Zechariah was written after Israel was allowed to return home from the Babylonian captivity.

The fact that these women are said to have "wings" has caused many people to view them as angels. Is this what the Bible is attempting to teach us in this passage? Are there are female angels?

There are a number of observations we need to make in answering this question.

ANGELS ALWAYS APPEAR TO HUMANS AS MEN AND WITHOUT WINGS

As we have previously mentioned, in the Bible when angels have appeared to humans, we are never told that they have wings. Instead, they always appear as normal looking men. While at times their clothing is dazzling, their appearance is consistently like that of a man. We find this taught throughout Scripture from the first page until the last.

THESE TWO FEMALES ARE NOT CALLED ANGELS

There is something else we must note. In this passage, these females are never called "angels." They are two wing-women who transport a basket that contains an evil woman to Babylonia. They are not described as messengers of God, or messengers of the devil for that matter.

THIS IS A VISION, NOT AN ACTUAL APPEARANCE OF ANGELS

Furthermore, this is a vision that we are dealing with in this context. In the first part of this chapter, Zechariah was shown a vision of a flying scroll. Now we have the vision of flying women with wings who flew the basket, containing an evil woman, to Babylonia.

In sum, since we are dealing with a vision, and not an actual appearance of an angel to humans, we should be careful about what conclusions we make. Indeed, since the Bible uniformly teaches that angels always appear as men, and never have wings, we should not assume that in this highly symbolic passage that female angels are in view here.

SUMMARY TO QUESTION 34
DOES THE BOOK OF ZECHARIAH SPEAK ABOUT FEMALE ANGELS?

When angels appear to people in the Bible they always appear as men. We find this consistently throughout the Scripture.

However, in the Book of Zechariah there is a description of two women with wings which transport a woman in a measuring basket to the land of Babylonia. The woman in the basket is designated as "wickedness."

The fact that these two women have wings, and they fly the basket to Babylon, has caused many to wonder if we have female angels in view here.

However, the evidence does not lead us to conclude that. In every other instance in the Bible, angels that visit humans are always male and never have wings. Furthermore, the women in this passage, though they are winged, are not called angels. Add to this the passage is a highly symbolic vision of what will take place in the future.

Consequently, there is not enough evidence from this passage to conclude that angels may appear as females.

QUESTION 35

Should People
Worship Angels?

When angels have appeared on the pages of Scripture, they often are impressive looking; large of stature and having clothing described as dazzling. Because of their imposing appearance, there was the temptation to worship them. Is it, therefore, legitimate to worship these heavenly beings?

WE ARE NOT TO WORSHIP ANGELS

Though impressive looking beings, angels should never be worshipped! Since God created angels as spirit-beings to minister to His people, they are not worthy to be worshipped. In fact, the Bible warns us against such practice.

1. JOHN WAS TOLD NOT TO WORSHIP AN ANGEL

There were two incidents when John the Apostle was rebuked when he attempted to worship an angel. We read the following in the Book of Revelation.

> Then I fell down at his feet to worship him, but he said, "No, don't worship me. For I am a servant of God, just like you and other brothers and sisters who testify of their faith in Jesus. Worship God. For the essence of prophecy is to give a clear witness for Jesus" (Revelation 19:10 NLT).

The angel made it clear that only God is worthy of our worship—we should not worship angels.

On another occasion, John again attempted to worship an angel. This is also recorded in the Book of Revelation.

> I, John, am the one who heard and saw these things. And when I heard and saw them, I fell down to worship at the feet of the angel who showed them to me; but he said to me, "You must not do that! I am a fellow servant with you and your comrades the prophets, and with those who keep the words of this book. Worship God!" (Revelation 22:8,9 NRSV).

Only God is to be worshipped, no other being is worthy.

2. ANGEL WORSHIP WAS PRACTICED AT THAT TIME

It seems that angel worship was practiced at the time Paul wrote to the Colossians. In fact, he warned the people about the worship of angels. He wrote.

> Do not let anyone disqualify you, insisting on self-abasement and worship of angels, dwelling on visions, puffed up without cause by a human way of thinking (Colossians 2:18 NRSV).

Paul forbade believers to be engaged in such conduct. Though we do not fully understand the background of his statements, several observations can be made.

A. THE PEOPLE HAD EXPERIENCED VISIONS

The people who were engaged in angel worship had experienced visions. They were dwelling on what these visions had told them.

In fact, the Bible warns people to beware of angels appearing to them. Paul wrote to the Galatians as follows.

But even if we, or an angel from heaven, preach any other gospel to you than what we have preached to you, let him be accursed. As we have said before, so now I say again, if anyone preaches any other gospel to you than what you have received, let him be accursed (Galatians 1:8,9 NKJV).

The fact that a person receives an angelic visit or vision does not make the event something that God has ordained. Indeed, they can present a false message.

B. THEY WERE FILLED WITH PRIDE

Those who practiced angel worship were lifted up with pride. Indeed, they considered themselves more holy than anyone else because of their angelic visions. Their pride, in turn, brought about a false humility. Though they were pretending to be humble, they were, in actuality, proud.

C. THEY FOCUSED ON ANGELS, NOT JESUS

These people had the wrong focus. They were dwelling on angels, instead of the Creator of angels, Jesus. This type of thinking was not divine, but rather human. For this, the Apostle Paul chastised them.

D. IT BROUGHT ABOUT NEGATIVE RESULTS

The worship of angels, therefore, can bring about a number of negative results. It was wrong from the start because it centered on the wrong object—the creation rather than the Creator.

From the very beginning, the Lord has emphasized that He and He alone is worthy of our worship. We read about this in the Ten Commandments.

Never have any other god. Never make your own carved idols or statues that represent any creature in the sky, on the earth, or in the water. Never worship them or serve them,

because I, the Lord your God, am a God who does not tolerate rivals (Exodus 20:3-5 God's Word).

Angel worship would certainly constitute a rival to the One True God.

IS THIS WHY ANGELS REMAIN INVISIBLE?

One of the possible reasons as to why angels remain invisible is that,
if visible, humans would worship them. As long as humanity cannot
see angels, or directly experience or contact them, then the chances of
angel worship is greatly diminished.

SUMMARY TO QUESTION 35
SHOULD PEOPLE WORSHIP ANGELS?

The worship of angels is something that is condemned in Scripture.
Only God is to be worshipped. The angels of God do not allow
themselves to be worshipped, they always direct worship to where it
belongs—to God and Him alone.

In fact, on two occasions, John the Apostle was rebuked by angels
when he attempted to worship them.

When Paul wrote to the Colossians he warned them about those who
worshipped angels. These people, who claimed to have had angelic
visions, were filled with pride. This is exactly the opposite behavior
that a believer in the Lord should exhibit.

Furthermore, worship of angels distracts us from the true object of our
worship, the God of the Bible. He and He alone should be worshipped.
Indeed, this is emphasized in the Ten Commandments where the Lord
forbids worship of anyone, or any thing, apart from Him.

In sum, for a number of reasons, angel worship is something which
should never be practiced.

Should We
Pray To Angels?

When we pray, should we ever address our prayers to angels? Can they answer our prayers? The Bible gives a clear, "No" to this question as to whom we should pray. We can observe what the Scripture says about this idea.

1. WE ARE TO PRAY TO GOD ALONE

The Bible says that prayers should be directed to God and to Him alone. Paul wrote to Timothy about this important truth. He stated it in this manner.

> For there is one God and one intermediary between God and humanity, Christ Jesus, himself human (1 Timothy 2:5 NET).

Note that here is only one intermediary, or go-between, between humanity and God—the Lord Jesus Christ. Angels, nor anyone else, can intercede for believers directly to God the Father. Only the Lord Jesus can do this.

2. ONLY GOD CAN HELP

Angels only serve to do the bidding of God. In fact, their mission is made clear by the writer to the Hebrews.

Are they not all ministering spirits, sent out to serve those who will inherit salvation (Hebrews 1:14 NET).

They only go where the Lord sends them. They cannot, in and of themselves, help us because their power is derived from God. Whenever they come to the aid of believers, it is because of the direct command of God.

Therefore it is worthless to call upon them to help us. Only the Lord can deliver His people. The psalmist wrote the Lord saying the following.

Call upon me in the day of trouble; I will deliver you, and you shall glorify me (Psalm 50:15 ESV).

God is the only one who can help us. This is a biblical truth that we should never ever forget. Indeed, He alone is our help and our strength. Therefore, we should never ask angels to help us, for they are cannot.

SUMMARY TO QUESTION 36
SHOULD WE PRAY TO ANGELS?

Never in Scripture do we find any example of people praying to angels. Angels are sent to do God's bidding in answer to prayer. Prayers are never directed toward them, and should never be.

Indeed, there is only one way in which we can have access to God the Father—through the person of Jesus Christ. There is no other way in which an individual can have their prayers answered.

In sum, angels do not serve any function as intermediaries between God and humanity in that sense. They do the bidding of God but only when the Lord sends them. In other words, since they never act on their own it is worthless to pray directly to them. They cannot help us.

QUESTION 37

Do Angels Appear
To People Today?

Is it possible for angels to appear to people today? Should we expect angelic visits? What do the Bible have to say about angels visiting humans?

ANGELS WERE NOT IMMEDIATELY RECOGNIZED ON A NUMBER OCCASIONS

Interestingly, we find that on several occasions, angels appeared in the form of men, to such a degree, that they were not at first identified as angels.

ABRAHAM

For example, Scripture says that the patriarch Abraham entertained "three men" as dinner guests in his tent on the plains of Mamre.

> The Lord appeared again to Abraham near the oak grove belonging to Mamre. One day Abraham was sitting at the entrance to his tent during the hottest part of the day. He looked up and noticed three men standing nearby. When he saw them, he ran to meet them and welcomed them, bowing low to the ground (Genesis 18:1-2 NLT).

One angel remained to talk with Abraham while the other "two angels" went on down to Sodom to visit his nephew Lot.

LOT

When they arrived, they spent the night with Lot, who thought at first they were men, not heavenly messengers

> The two angels came to Sodom in the evening while Lot was sitting in the city's gateway. When Lot saw them, he got up to meet them and bowed down with his face toward the ground. He said, "Here, my lords, please turn aside to your servant's house. Stay the night and wash your feet. Then you can be on your way early in the morning." "No," they replied, "we'll spend the night in the town square" (Genesis 19:1,2 NET).

Lot thought he was showing hospitality to two men.

Therefore, on each of these occasions, the angelic visitors, were not immediately recognized as angels. They were first perceived as mere men.

SCRIPTURE ACKNOWLEDGES THAT PEOPLE ENTERTAINED ANGELS WITHOUT IMMEDIATELY REALIZING IT

The Bible does speak of humans entertaining angelic visitors without being aware.

> Let brotherly love continue. Don't neglect to show hospitality, for by doing this some have welcomed angels as guests without knowing it (Hebrews 13:1,2 HCSB).

According to this passage, it was possible for angels to appear to humans without anyone being aware it was actually angels. As we have noted, this is exactly what happened to Abraham and Lot.

Since angels have done so in the past, as we have just observed, there is nothing impossible about this happening today.

GOD WORKS AS HE DESIRES

Jesus made it clear that God works as He desires. When He spoke to the religious leader Nicodemus, Jesus made the following statement about how the Spirit of God works.

> The wind blows where it wishes, and you hear the sound of it, but cannot tell where it comes from and where it goes. So is everyone who is born of the Spirit (John 3:8 NKJV).

Therefore the visitation of an angel is certainly possible, if God so desires.

THIS WAS NOT NORMAL IN BIBLICAL TIMES

However, we must also recognize that angelic appearances were not normal in biblical times. As we look at the entire scope of biblical history, we find very few examples of angels appearing to humans. In other words, angelic appearances were the exception rather than the rule. Consequently, it is certainly not something that normally happened to biblical characters.

THE ACTIVITY OF ANGELS HAS BEEN SUPERSEDED BY THE WORK OF THE HOLY SPIRIT

There is one final thing that we should note. For those who have believed in Jesus, the activity of angels, as revealed in the Bible, has now been superseded by the work of the Holy Spirit.

According to Jesus, He is the One who now guides believers into "all truth." On the night of His betrayal, the Lord said the following to His disciples.

> I have many more things to say to you, but you cannot bear them now. But when he, the Spirit of truth, comes, he will guide you into all truth. For he will not speak on his own authority, but will speak whatever he hears, and will tell you what is to come (John 16:12,13 NET).

Therefore, while angels still carry on their work, for the believer, our guidance comes from God the Holy Spirit living inside of each and every one of us. In other words, we should not be looking to angels to gives us personal guidance in our lives.

SUMMARY TO QUESTION 37
DO ANGELS APPEAR TO PEOPLE TODAY?

Angelic visits have happened in the past. The Scriptures give many examples of this. On certain occasions the people were unaware of the angelic appearance. This is true in the case of the three angels who appeared to Abraham as men. Two of them went ahead to Sodom and appeared to Lot. At first, neither man recognized these visitors as angels.

God works any way that He desires. Consequently, there is certainly nothing stopping Him from sending an angelic visitor to someone today, if He should so wish.

Yet we must remember that angelic appearances were not the norm in biblical times. Indeed, they only appeared to humans on rare occasions and each time they did appear it was at a critical juncture in biblical history.

There is one final thing that we do know. Today, it is the Holy Spirit of God who guides the believers, who leads us into the truth of God. Therefore, we should not be looking for angelic guidance or angelic appearances. The role of guiding the believer is that of the Holy Spirit.

Therefore believers should not expect angels to appear to them.

QUESTION 38

Do Believers Have
A Guardian Angel?

People often wonder if they have a guardian angel looking after them. Is there a special angel assigned to each person? What does the Bible say?

JESUS' STATEMENT ABOUT ANGELS

In the gospels, we find that Jesus made a statement which seems to teach that believes have guardian angels. Matthew records Him saying the following.

> Take care that you do not despise one of these little ones; for, I tell you, in heaven their angels continually see the face of my Father in heaven (Matthew 18:10 NRSV).

This has caused some to think that each believer has a special angel looking after them. A number of observations should be made.

1. ANGELS DO PROTECT

We do know that one of the ministries of angels is to protect God's people. The psalmist wrote.

> The angel of the LORD encamps around those who fear him, and delivers them (Psalm 34:7 NRSV).

The psalmist wrote elsewhere of the protection of angels.

> For he orders his angels to protect you wherever you go. They
> will hold you with their hands to keep you from striking
> your foot on a stone (Psalm 91:11,12 NLT).

Angels have the job of protection.

2. THEY BELIEVERS SPOKE OF PETER'S ANGEL

There is an incident, found in the Book of Acts, which may indicate
that the early church understood Jesus' words to mean that believers
have guardian angels.

When Peter escaped from prison, he came to the place where the
believers were praying for his release. When he knocked at the door,
the servant girl saw it was Peter, and told the others. They responded
in this manner.

> "You're crazy!" they told her. But she kept insisting that it
> was true. Then they said, "It's his angel!" (Acts 12:15 HCSB).

Instead of thinking it was actually Peter, some thought that it was his
angel. This may provide some evidence that they believed Peter actually
had an angel guarding him.

THIS IS NOT NECESSARILY TRUE

While this may teach us that each believer has a guardian angel, this
is not necessarily the case. Jesus taught that multitudes of angels were
at His disposal when He was betrayed in the Garden of Gethsemane.

> Then some men came forward, took hold of Jesus, and
> arrested him. Suddenly, one of the men with Jesus pulled
> out his sword and cut off the ear of the chief priest's ser-
> vant. Then Jesus said to him, "Put your sword away!
> All who use a sword will be killed by a sword. Don't you

think that I could call on my Father to send more than twelve legions of angels to help me now? How, then, are the Scriptures to be fulfilled that say this must happen" (Matthew 26:50-54 God's Word).

This also seems to be the case with each believer—multitudes of angels are at our disposal. The Bible says the following of them.

> But to which of the angels has he ever said, "Sit at my right hand until I make your enemies a footstool for your feet"? Are they not all ministering spirits, sent out to serve those who will inherit salvation (Hebrews 1:13,14 NET).

We are told that angels are ministering spirits who are sent to do the work of the Lord. Therefore, we should not assume that we merely have one of them looking after us.

In fact, the Bible says that Elisha the prophet prayed that his servant would see the angels that were present when he was surrounded by troops, chariots, and horses.

> When the servant of the man of God got up and went out early the next morning, an army with horses and chariots had surrounded the city. "Oh no, my lord! What shall we do?" the servant asked. "Don't be afraid," the prophet answered. "Those who are with us are more than those who are with them." And Elisha prayed, "Open his eyes, Lord, so that he may see." Then the Lord opened the servant's eyes, and he looked and saw the hills full of horses and chariots of fire all around Elisha. As the enemy came down toward him, Elisha prayed to the Lord, "Strike this army with blindness." So he struck them with blindness, as Elisha had asked (2 Kings 6:15-18 NIV).

In this instance, the multitude of angels, called "chariots of fire" here, intervened and struck the enemies with blindness.

THE HOLY SPIRIT INDWELLS ALL BELIEVERS

There is something else. The Bible teaches that God the Holy Spirit indwells all believers. Jesus said.

And I will ask the Father, and he will give you another Counselor, who will never leave you (John 14:16 NLT).

If the Holy Spirit of God resides inside each believer, then one might ask, "Why would we need a guardian angel looking after us?"

Therefore, a single guardian angel for each believer seems to be unnecessary.

SUMMARY TO QUESTION 38
DO BELIEVERS HAVE A GUARDIAN ANGEL?

Jesus spoke of angels guarding each believer. Whether each Christian has only one angel looking after them, or a vast number of angels, the Bible does not specifically say.

Based on the passage in Hebrews, it may be more proper to say that believers have a number of angels that are looking out for their interests. We do know that angels offer protection to Christians.

In fact, we find that Elisha the prophet asked the Lord to open the eyes of his servant when they were surrounded by troops, chariots, and horses. The servant was then allowed to see an army of angels protecting them. In fact, these angels struck the enemy troops with blindness.

And one last thing, since God's Spirit lives inside each believer the need for a guardian angel may not be that necessary.

QUESTION 39

Does Each Church Have An Individual Angel Watching Over It?

There is a statement found in the Book of Revelation that some Bible students believe may teach that each individual church has an angel watching over it. The statement reads as follows.

> The secret of the seven stars you saw in My right hand, and of the seven gold lampstands, is this: the seven stars are the angels of the seven churches, and the seven lampstands are the seven churches. "To the angel of the church in Ephesus write: "The One who holds the seven stars in His right hand and who walks among the seven gold lampstands says" (Revelation 1:20, 2:1 HCSB).

It is argued that the "angel" referred to here may represent an individual heavenly being that protects and watches over each church. Yet this is not possible from the context.

These same angels that carried the message to the various churches are included in the rebuke of Jesus. They participated in the same sinful conduct as the churches to whom the messages were brought. They are also urged to repent.

> But I have this against you: You have abandoned the love you had at first. Remember then how far you have fallen; repent, and do the works you did at first. Otherwise, I will come to

229

you and remove your lampstand from its place—unless you repent (Revelation 2:4,5 HCSB).

Since good angels do not sin, nor do they have any need of repenting, this rules them out as the persons described in this passage. Other solutions will need to be found for the identity of these angels.

THERE ARE A GREAT NUMBER OF ANGELS

Instead of one particular angel watching over each church, it seems more consistent with Scripture that each church has a great number of angels watching over them. The Apostle Paul wrote to Timothy.

I solemnly charge you before God and Christ Jesus and the elect angels to observe these things without prejudice, doing nothing out of favoritism (1 Timothy 5:21 HCSB).

Paul indicated that many angels are watching what goes on in the church. He wrote the following to the believers in Corinth.

For this reason the woman ought to have a symbol of authority on her head, because of the angels (1 Corinthians 11:10 NKJV).

The angels are observing what is going on with the believers.

To conclude, rather than one particular angel looking after each assembly of believers it is possible that there are many angels who are at the ready to help if necessary.

SUMMARY TO QUESTION 39
DOES EACH CHURCH HAVE AN INDIVIDUAL ANGEL WATCHING OVER IT?

While it is possible that each church has a special angel looking over it, the word translated "angel" in Revelation 2 and 3 cannot refer to such beings. The angels, or "messengers," under consideration here are included in the sinful deeds of the churches to whom they bring the message of Christ. They are also commanded to repent. Since good angels do not sin, or need to repent for their sins, some other persons must be in view in this passage.

Scripture also hints that a number of angels are watching over each church, rather than one individual angel. However, there is no specific passage that makes this clear one way or the other.

Do Angels Transport Believers At Death?

It is a very popular idea that angels carry believers into God's presence upon their death. Does the Bible teach that angels transport believers when they die?

BELIEVERS ARE IMMEDIATELY WITH CHRIST

The Bible teaches that those who die in Christ are immediately brought into His presence. Paul wrote the following to the Corinthians.

> And we are confident and satisfied to be out of the body and at home with the Lord (2 Corinthians 5:8 HCSB).

Being absent from the body means being immediately with the Lord. This is indeed a wonderful promise!

THE DEAD MAN LAZARUS WAS BROUGHT BY ANGELS

It seems that angels are the ones who transport believers into God's presence. Jesus asserted this in a story that He told.

> One day the poor man died and was carried away by the angels to Abraham's side. The rich man also died and was buried (Luke 16:22 HCSB).

According to this passage, when believers die, angels bring them into God's presence. Since angels are called ministering spirits, the transporting of the believing dead seems to be one of their ministries. Though this is the only passage in Scripture that speaks to this subject, there is no indication that this example is an abnormal occurrence.

Today, when a believer dies, we may assume that angels bring them into the presence of the Lord. What we do know is this: once a believer dies they are immediately ushered into His presence.

SUMMARY TO QUESTION 40
DO ANGELS TRANSPORT BELIEVERS AT DEATH?

We know from Scripture that the moment a believer dies they go immediately to be with the Lord. There are a number of passages that indicate this.

We also find Jesus telling the story of angels transporting a poor man named Lazarus at his death into the presence of the Lord. Though this is the only passage in the Bible that deals with this subject, it does seem to teach that this is one of the many ministries of angels.

Therefore, today when a believer dies, it is possible that angels bring them into the presence of the Lord. Whether or not we are brought there by angels, we are indeed brought into His presence the moment that we die.

In What Sense Will
Believers Judge Angels?

The Bible says that believers will indeed judge angels. We read of this in Paul's letter to the Corinthians when he stated the following.

> Do you not know that we shall judge angels? How much more, things that pertain to this life? (1 Corinthians 6:3 NKJV).

The judgment of angels is something that has been given to believers. Though human beings have been made a little lower than the angels in their nature, those who have trusted the Lord will be given the responsibility of judging angels in the age to come.

THE NATURE OF JUDGING IS NOT STATED

The nature of the judgment of the angels is not stated, but judgment does not necessarily imply condemnation. Since the good angels do not sin, there is nothing for which to condemn them.

THIS MAY INVOLVE RULERSHIP IN THE KINGDOM

The judgment of angels, if the righteous angels are in mind, most likely has to do with rulership in the kingdom. The Bible teaches that believers will be rulers over different aspects of the kingdom of God. Jesus made this clear in one of His parables.

His master said to him, 'Well done, good and trustworthy slave; you have been trustworthy in a few things, I will put you in charge of many things; enter into the joy of your master' (Matthew 25:23 NRSV).

Faithfulness in small things, will allow believers to rule over many things. Angels will be included in this sphere of rulership.

THERE IS NO EVIDENCE THAT BELIEVERS WILL CONDEMN EVIL ANGELS

What about the idea that believers will judge evil angels? Can this be what the passage is speaking about?

As we search the Scriptures we find nothing that indicates that believers will stand in condemnation of the evil angels. At the Great White Throne judgment, the Lord is the One who will condemn all who are lost. The Bible puts it this way.

Then I saw a great white throne and Him who sat on it, from whose face the earth and the heaven fled away. And there was found no place for them (Revelation 20:11 NKJV).

It is the Lord who will condemn the lost. This is not the task of believers. The Lord, and He alone, will do this.

SUMMARY TO QUESTION 41
IN WHAT SENSE WILL BELIEVERS JUDGE ANGELS?

The judgment of angels is something that has been committed to believers. However, nowhere in the Scripture is it explained. Since it seems to be the good angels we will judge, the nature of the judgment will be one of rulership, not of condemnation. Redeemed believers will exercise authority over the angels in the ages to come.

There is no scriptural basis that believers will stand in condemnation of evil angels. That is the Lord's responsibility, and His alone.

What Do The Books Written Between The Testaments Have To Say About Angels?

Between the time after the Old Testament was completed, and the time when the Lord again spoke to the people, about four hundred years elapsed. During that period, a number of Jewish writings were produced.

While these works were not divinely inspired Scripture, they do reflect the thoughts and feelings of the people at that time. In these works a number of references to angels are found.

It seems that what was written between the testaments had some influence on those living at the time of Christ. Therefore, it will be profitable to discover exactly what was written and taught about angels during this period.

MANY THINGS WERE TAUGHT ABOUT ANGELS

A number of things were taught about angels during this time. For example, there were assumed to be seven archangels or chief angels. Among those named were Michael, Gabriel, Uriel, and Raphael. Only Michael and Gabriel are mentioned by name in Scripture. However, Gabriel is never called an archangel. Michael is called an archangel, but not in the Old Testament.

A few other things of interest should be noted.

GABRIEL

According to 2 Enoch 24:1, Gabriel sat on God's left side, while Michael sat on God's right hand side. Michael was supposedly concerned with the affairs in heaven while Gabriel was given charge of affairs on the earth. Nothing like this is taught in Scripture.

RAPHAEL

According to the apocryphal book of Tobit, Raphael presented the prayers of godly Jews to the Lord.

> I am Raphael, one of the seven angels who stand ready and enter before the glory of the Lord (Tobit 12:15 NRSV).

This assumes that the prayers of believes are presented to the Lord by an angelic messenger. Again, this is something that is not taught in Scripture.

URIEL

Uriel was the angel who explained to Enoch many of his visions. This includes the fate of the fallen angels who married earthly women. These are found in the Book of First Enoch.

Uriel also interpreted Ezra's vision of the heavenly Jerusalem. This is found in 2 Esdras 10:28-57. As mentioned, no such angels named Raphael or Uriel are revealed in Scripture and there is no convincing evidence whatsoever that fallen angels had ever married earthly women.

THESE FOUR ANGELS REPORT TO GOD

In First Enoch, these four archangels reported to God about how depraved the human race had become. God then instructed them on what they were to do. They were given an assignment on how to remedy the situation.

This gives us a sample of how angels were seen in the period between the testaments.

DID THIS AFFECT THE NEW TESTAMENT BELIEF?

There are some who contend that the teachings about angels between the testaments actually affected the beliefs of some New Testament writers.

However, this is not necessary to conclude. Everything that is taught about the nature of angels in the New Testament is consistent with that which has been revealed in the Old Testament.

Yet, it is possible that those who wrote between the testaments may have had some access to divinely revealed truths that God's spokesmen, the prophets, proclaimed.

For some reason, what they said was not recorded for us. We know that most of the things they did preach and teach were not recorded.

Thus, it is not impossible that some of these traditions about angels were actually taught by God's designated spokesmen but never recorded for us in the Bible. However of this we cannot be certain.

SUMMARY TO QUESTION 42
WHAT DO THE BOOKS WRITTEN BETWEEN THE TESTAMENTS HAVE TO SAY ABOUT ANGELS?

Between the testaments there were developments in the beliefs about angels. Seven archangels are mentioned as existing and various duties are assigned to them. While certain information about angels that is revealed between the testaments is not found in written Scripture, we cannot be absolutely certain that some of the truths may have been orally proclaimed by God's prophets. There is insufficient information to be certain.

QUESTION 43

What Observations And Conclusions Should We Make About Angels?

Having looked at the biblical teaching on the subject of the good angels, we can make the following conclusions.

OBSERVATION 1: ANGELS DO EXIST

From the first book of the Bible until the last we know that angels do indeed exist. There is no doubt about this whatsoever.

While angels do exist, and appear often in Scripture, there is much that we do not know about them. The main reason for this is that the Bible is not that concerned about them. Instead, it is concerned about God and us! Indeed, the story of the Bible is God's dealings with humanity, in particular those who have placed their faith in Him.

OBSERVATION 2: THEY ARE INVISIBLE TO HUMANS

Angels are spirit-beings, invisible to the human eyes. While there are a few occasions in which they have been made visible to humans, they constantly minister in the realm that is invisible to us. Therefore, we only know about them through divine revelation.

OBSERVATION 3: THEY MINISTER TO THE PEOPLE OF GOD

The ministry of angels is to the people of God, it is not to unbelievers. Indeed, they are called "ministering spirits" to help those who are heirs of salvation. In other words, unbelievers never receive angelic visitation.

OBSERVATION 4: THEY ARE SEXLESS, DEATHLESS CREATURES

Although angels always appear to people as males, they are neither male nor female. In fact, they are sexless, deathless creatures. They do not have families, they do not age.

OBSERVATION 5: THEY ARE INNUMERABLE

The number of angels is countless. However, their number seems to be fixed. In other words, they will not increase unless the Lord decides to create more of them. Neither can they decrease.

OBSERVATION 6: THEY PRESENTLY ARE A HIGHER ORDER OF BEING THAN HUMANS

Today, they are a higher order of being than humans. Scripture makes it clear that humans were made a little lower than the angels. Consequently, we should view them as more wise and powerful than us.

However, there are other beings in heaven which the Lord created, the cherubim, seraphim, and the living creatures, that seemingly rank higher than the angels. Indeed, with the one exception of the cherubim guarding the Garden of Eden after the sin of Adam and Eve, these other beings remain in heaven. In contrast to them are the angels who are messengers sent to do the will of God.

OBSERVATION 7: SOMEDAY HUMANS WILL JUDGE ANGELS

There will come a time when believers will judge angels. This will involve the righteous angels, not the evil ones. The judgment is not in a condemning sense but rather it will probably have something to do with overseeing and rulership in the kingdom.

These are some of the truths we learn about angels from the Word of God. While there is much we know about them, there remains much that we still do not know.

SUMMARY TO QUESTION 43
WHAT OBSERVATIONS AND CONCLUSIONS SHOULD WE MAKE ABOUT ANGELS?

After examining what the Bible has to say about the subject of angels there are a number of observations and conclusions that we can make.

First, angels do exist. Scripture makes this clear. In fact, we find that they have been very active during the biblical period. Indeed, from the Book of Genesis through the Book of Revelation we find angels appearing to humans.

Angels are invisible beings. Unless the Lord allows them to be seen by us, they will remain unseen. When they do appear to humans, it is always as males. They never appear as female or as children.

Since angels are spirit beings they have no physical form, at least not like us. God also is spirit and Scripture says that He does not have any physical form either.

Angels do not marry, they do not have families. They are sexless, death-less beings. Their number can never decrease. Of course, they could increase if the Lord decided to create more of them.

Angels were created to assist believers. They are called ministering spirits. They do not help unbelievers.

Angels were created as a higher order of being than humans. The Bible tells us that human beings were made a little lower than the angels. However, angels may not be the highest order of created beings. The Scripture speaks of the cherubim, seraphim, and living creatures. They all seem to rank higher in the heavenly realm than the angels.

While humans now rank below the angels, there will come a day when we will judge angels. This, most likely, has to do with rulership in the kingdom of God. In other words, we will judge the righteous angels in the sense that we will rule over them. Nothing is stated in the Bible concerning humans judging the evil angels. That responsibility belongs to the Lord and to Him alone.

This briefly sums up what Scripture has to say about these invisible spirit-beings which the Lord created to assist believers.

How Has The Lord Used Angels To Announce Future Events As Well As Forewarning Of Judgment?

The work, or ministry, of angels, with respect to humanity, can be placed in a number of different categories. This includes announcing future events, as well as forewarning people about coming judgment and potential disasters. We can cite the following examples.

ANGELS HAVE ANNOUNCED IMPORTANT BIRTHS

On some very special occasions, the Lord has sent his angel to announce the births of certain children. As we will discover, each of these births played a crucial role in the overall plan of God.

THE BIRTH OF ISAAC IS ANNOUNCED BY AN ANGEL

An angel announced in advance to Abraham and Sarah the conception and birth of their son Isaac. The Bible explains what happened in this manner.

> They said to him, "Where is Sarah your wife?" And he said, "She is in the tent." The Lord said, "I will surely return to you about this time next year, and Sarah your wife shall have a son." And Sarah was listening at the tent door behind him (Genesis 18: 9-10 ESV).

The prediction of the angel, who appeared in the form of a man, came to pass. Though Abraham and Sarah were past the age of childbearing, Isaac was miraculously born to them. Consequently, the chosen people, Israel, had a supernatural beginning which was announced beforehand by an angel.

THE BIRTH OF SAMSON WAS FORETOLD

The Bible says that an angel foretold the birth of Samson to his parents. We read how an angel appeared to his mother.

> And the angel of the Lord appeared to the woman and said to her, "Behold, you are barren and have not borne children, but you shall conceive and bear a son. Therefore be careful and drink no wine or strong drink, and eat nothing unclean" (Judges 13:3,4 ESV).

Samson was representative of the various "Judges" which the Lord sent to the people of Israel during a very dark period of their history. The birth of this "deliverer" was foretold.

THE PARENTS OF JOHN THE BAPTIST WERE TOLD THAT THEY WOULD HAVE A SON

Before his wife Elizabeth became pregnant, the angel Gabriel announced the birth of John the Baptist to his father Zechariah. Scripture records the response of Zechariah to this.

> Zechariah was shaken and overwhelmed with fear when he saw him. But the angel said, "Don't be afraid, Zechariah! God has heard your prayer. Your wife, Elizabeth, will give you a son, and you are to name him John" (Luke 1:13 NLT).

John the Baptist was a key figure in biblical history. Indeed, after a four hundred year silence, the New Testament era began with the visit of the angel Gabriel to Zechariah. The child would be the forerunner of the Messiah. The salvation of the Lord was about to come to the world!

246

JESUS' BIRTH WAS FORETOLD BY AN ANGEL

The birth of Jesus the Messiah to Mary, before she was with child, was also announced by the angel Gabriel. Scripture explains it this way.

> "Don't be afraid, Mary," the angel told her, "for you have found favor with God! You will conceive and give birth to a son, and you will name him Jesus" (Luke 1:30 NLT).

Not only was Jesus' birth foretold by an angel, on the night that He was born, His birth was announced by an angel to the shepherds. Instantly, we find that a heavenly choir of angels began to praise God concerning this blessed event.

> That night there were shepherds staying in the fields nearby, guarding their flocks of sheep. Suddenly, an angel of the Lord appeared among them, and the radiance of the Lord's glory surrounded them. They were terrified, but the angel reassured them. "Don't be afraid!" he said. "I bring you good news that will bring great joy to all people. The Savior—yes, the Messiah, the Lord—has been born today in Bethlehem, the city of David! And you will recognize him by this sign: You will find a baby wrapped snugly in strips of cloth, lying in a manger." Suddenly, the angel was joined by a vast host of others—the armies of heaven—praising God and saying, "Glory to God in highest heaven, and peace on earth to those with whom God is pleased (Luke 2: 8-14 NLT).

Angels rejoiced at the birth of the Lord.

These five occasions marked important events in the history of God's dealing with the human race. Consequently, the Lord sent His angel to announce these special births.

ANGELS HAVE FOREWARNED ABOUT COMING DISASTERS

While angels have been sent to announce special births, the Bible also tells us that angels have announced impending disasters that were about to occur. We can cite the following examples.

ANGELS WARNED ABOUT THE COMING DESTRUCTION OF SODOM

Abraham and Lot were forewarned by angels of the destruction of the evil cities of Sodom and Gomorrah. The Lord, through His angel, said the following to Abraham.

> Then the Lord said, "Because the outcry against Sodom and Gomorrah is great and their sin is very grave, I will go down to see whether they have done altogether according to the outcry that has come to me. And if not, I will know" (Genesis 18:20,21 ESV).

Later two angels, appearing as men, told Lot to leave the city of Sodom because of its imminent destruction.

> Then the men said to Lot, "Have you anyone else here? Sons-in-law, sons, daughters, or anyone you have in the city, bring them out of the place. For we are about to destroy this place, because the outcry against its people has become great before the Lord, and the Lord has sent us to destroy it" (Genesis 19:12-13 ESV).

As the angels predicted, the wicked city of Sodom was destroyed.

JOSEPH WAS WARNED TO TAKE THE BABY JESUS AWAY FROM BETHLEHEM

In the New Testament, Joseph was warned by an angel to take Mary and the baby Jesus away from the city of Bethlehem.

> Now when they had departed, behold, an angel of the Lord appeared to Joseph in a dream and said, "Rise, take the child and his mother, and flee to Egypt, and remain there until I tell you, for Herod is about to search for the child, to destroy him" (Matthew 2:13 ESV).

The warning of the angel was heeded by Joseph. Indeed, it averted a disaster.

Later, the same angel told Joseph that it was time to return from Egypt.

> After Herod had died, an angel of the Lord appeared in a dream to Joseph in Egypt saying, "Get up, take the child and his mother, and go to the land of Israel, for those who were seeking the child's life are dead" (Matthew 2:19 NET).

Joseph obeyed. He brought Mary and the child Jesus back to the land of Israel having escaped the murderous plans of Herod.

ANGELS FOREWARN JUDGMENT IN THE BOOK OF REVELATION

Throughout the book of Revelation, we find a number of visitations by angels which forewarned about the coming judgment.

For example, we find that an angel will circle the earth warning the inhabitants of God's impending judgment.

> Then I saw another angel flying in midair, and he had the eternal gospel to proclaim to those who live on the earth— to every nation, tribe, language and people. He said in a loud voice, "Fear God and give him glory, because the hour of his judgment has come. Worship him who made the heavens, the earth, the sea and the springs of water" (Revelation 14:,6,7 NIV).

In this angelic announcement of the coming judgment there will be a message of hope for those who will turn to the Lord.

Like Sodom and Gomorrah at the beginning of Scripture, at the very end of the Bible we continue to find angels warning of God's impending judgment.

In sum, one of the many ministries of angels has been the announcement of important events before they take place. This includes significant births as well as announcing impending catastrophes.

SUMMARY TO APPENDIX 1
HOW HAS THE LORD USED ANGELS TO ANNOUNCE FUTURE EVENTS AS WELL AS FOREWARNING OF JUDGMENT?

Among the ministry of angels is the announcement of future events. Indeed, we find in two specific areas in which the Lord has used angels to make important announcements.

First, we find four significant births announced by angels. This includes the birth of Isaac to Abraham and Sarah, the birth of Samson to his parents, that of John the Baptist to his father Zechariah, and finally the announcement of the angel to Mary of the birth of Jesus the Messiah. Each of these births were turning points in the plan of God for the salvation of His people. The importance of each event is why an angel was sent to announce these births ahead of time. The Bible also records angels making an announcement at the birth of Jesus.

In addition, we find that angels, at certain times, forewarning of God's impending judgment as well as warning about potential disasters.

Abraham and Lot were warned about the coming judgment upon the evil cities of Sodom and Gomorrah. The family of Lot was able to escape because of the angelic warning.

Joseph, the husband of Mary, was warned by an angel about Herod's plot to kill the baby Jesus. He averted this by taking the Holy Family to Egypt.

Finally, John in the Book of Revelation, tells us that an angel will warn the inhabitants of the earth of God's impending judgment. This gives them a chance to repent and believe in Jesus before God's judgment arrives.

Therefore, angels have been used by the Lord on these occasions to both announce special births as well as to forewarn about coming disasters.

Did The Son Of God Appear To Daniel As An Angel? (Daniel 10:1-6)

At a crucial time in the history of Israel, there was an angelic visit to the prophet Daniel. This particular visit has caused certain commentators to believe that it was actually God the Son, the pre-incarnate Christ, who was this heavenly messenger. The Bible records what took place as follows.

> In the third year of Cyrus king of Persia, a revelation was given to Daniel (who was called Belteshazzar). Its message was true and it concerned a great war. The understanding of the message came to him in a vision. At that time I, Daniel, mourned for three weeks. I ate no choice food; no meat or wine touched my lips; and I used no lotions at all until the three weeks were over. On the twenty-fourth day of the first month, as I was standing on the bank of the great river, the Tigris, I looked up and there before me was a man dressed in linen, with a belt of fine gold from Uphaz around his waist. His body was like topaz, his face like lightning, his eyes like flaming torches, his arms and legs like the gleam of burnished bronze, and his voice like the sound of a multitude (Daniel 10:1-6 NIV).

After three weeks of fasting, when the prophet was standing by the Tigris River, he was visited by a messenger. Though he appeared as a man, this particular messenger was from heaven, he was not a human being. This personage was dressed in linen, had a dazzlingly bright appearance, and spoke with a powerful voice.

WHO WAS THIS PERSON?

Who was this personage that is described in this verse? Was is a mighty angel or was it God Himself, the pre-incarnate Christ, who appeared? Believers are divided on this question.

We will examine the arguments given for each view and then make some concluding observations.

VIEW 1: THE PERSONAGE WAS THE SON OF GOD

Many Bible students believe this person was God the Son, the pre-incarnate Christ. The reasons for this view are as follows.

THE SIMILARITIES BETWEEN THIS EPISODE AND OTHER APPEARANCES OF THE PRE-INCARNATE CHRIST

The similarities between this man, and the visions of Ezekiel and the Apostle John, argue for this being God the Son.

THE EXPERIENCE OF DANIEL WAS LIKE THAT OF EZEKIEL

The prophet Ezekiel had a vision of a man who had the appearance of the glory of the Lord.

> Then there was a voice from above the platform over their heads when they stood still. Above the platform over their heads was something like a sapphire shaped like a throne. High above on the throne was a form that appeared to be a man. I saw an amber glow like a fire enclosed all around from his waist up. From his waist down I saw something that looked like fire. There was a brilliant light around it, like the appearance of a rainbow in the clouds after the rain. This was

the appearance of the surrounding brilliant light; it looked like the glory of the Lord. When I saw it, I threw myself face down, and I heard a voice speaking (Ezekiel 1:25-28 NET).

Ezekiel described his encounter with this heavenly being. The prophet stated clearly what he saw, it was the appearance of the likeness of the glory of the Lord. The same glory of the Lord is referred to 16 times in the Book of Ezekiel (1:28; 3:12, 23; 8:4; 9:3; 10:4, 18- 19; 11:22- 23; 39:21; 43:2 [twice], 4-5; 44:4). There is no doubt that Ezekiel had a vision of the Lord.

Note that Ezekiel used the terms "appearance" and "likeness" when describing what he saw. The prophet was emphasizing that he had not seen God directly. Indeed, from other passages in Scripture we know that this would have caused his immediate death. However, it is clear that Ezekiel saw the likeness of God Himself in this vision.

Ezekiel's description of this "heavenly man" is similar to the one Daniel gives in this passage under consideration. Therefore, many people equate the two.

THE VISION OF JOHN

The Apostle John described a similar scene when he was taken up to heaven.

> After these things I looked, and there was a door standing open in heaven! And the first voice I had heard speaking to me like a trumpet said: "Come up here so that I can show you what must happen after these things." Immediately I was in the Spirit, and a throne was standing in heaven with someone seated on it! And the one seated on it was like jasper and carnelian in appearance, and a rainbow looking like it was made of emerald encircled the throne (Revelation 4:3 NET).

John also saw someone seated on the throne in heaven. When we couple Ezekiel's description of the man he saw, with John's similar description of the throne in heaven, it is clear that they each saw a vision of God Himself.

DANIEL'S EXPERIENCE WAS LIKE THAT OF SAUL OF TARSUS

There is a further reason to assume that Daniel was visited by the pre-incarnate Christ. Indeed, his experience was similar to that of Saul of Tarsus, when the resurrected Christ appeared to this persecutor of Christians while on the road to Damascus. Saul, who became Paul, explained it this way.

> King Agrippa, while on the road at midday, I saw a light from heaven brighter than the sun, shining around me and those traveling with me. We all fell to the ground, and I heard a voice speaking to me in the Hebrew language, 'Saul, Saul, why are you persecuting Me? It is hard for you to kick against the goads' (Acts 26:13,14 HCSB).

Paul explained that those who were with him heard a voice but did not understand what it was saying.

> Those who were with me saw the light, but did not understand the voice of the one who was speaking to me (Acts 22:9 NET).

Consequently, the men who were with Saul did not see the vision, nor did they understand the voice that was speaking with him when they all fell to the ground.

WE READ THAT SOMETHING SIMILAR HAPPENED TO DANIEL.

> Only I, Daniel, saw the vision. The men who were with me did not see it, but a great terror fell on them, and they ran and hid (Daniel 10:7 HCSB).

The connection between these two visions is obvious. Only Saul and Daniel saw the vision and understood the words of the Lord.

THE DESCRIPTION REMINDS US OF WHAT JOHN SAW

The description of the man which Daniel saw also reminds us of the description of the Lord Jesus in Revelation 1. John recorded what he saw as follows.

> And among the lampstands was One like the Son of Man, dressed in a long robe and with a gold sash wrapped around His chest. His head and hair were white like wool—white as snow—and His eyes like a fiery flame. His feet were like fine bronze as it is fired in a furnace, and His voice like the sound of cascading waters. He had seven stars in His right hand; a sharp double-edged sword came from His mouth, and His face was shining like the sun at midday (Revelation 1:13-16 HCSB).

This was the Son of God which John saw, as the Lord Himself later confirmed.

> Write to the angel of the church in Thyatira: The Son of God, the One whose eyes are like a fiery flame and whose feet are like fine bronze, says (Revelation 2:18 HCSB).

When the Apostle John saw the glorified Christ as recorded in the book of Revelation, he fell at His feet as though dead. The Lord told him not to be afraid.

> When I saw him I fell down at his feet as though I were dead, but he placed his right hand on me and said: "Do not be afraid! I am the first and the last, and the one who lives! I was dead, but look, now I am alive- forever and ever-and I hold the keys of death and of Hades! (Revelation 1:17,18 NET).

Something similar was told to Daniel. Indeed, he too was told not to be afraid.

> Then a hand touched me and set me on my hands and knees
> . . . When he said this to me, I stood up shaking. Then he
> said to me, "Don't be afraid" (Daniel 10:10,12 NET).

Again, the similarities between the two accounts is obvious.

These facts have led many to conclude that Daniel was visited by the pre-incarnate Christ.

VIEW 2: THE PERSONAGE WAS A MIGHTY ANGEL

While there are arguments that seem to link this messenger with God himself, in particular the pre-incarnate Christ, there are at least four main problems with this viewpoint.

For one thing, later in the passage we have a further description of this heavenly being as well as his mission. Indeed, he described to Daniel what took him so long to answer Daniel's prayer.

> But the prince of the Persian kingdom resisted me twenty-
> one days. Then Michael, one of the chief princes, came to
> help me, because I was detained there with the king of Persia
> (Daniel 10:13 NIV).

The words of this speaker rule out the possibility of him being the pre-incarnate Christ.

First there is the implausibility of God the Son being hindered by a demon, the prince of Persia. As the all-powerful Creator of all the angels, there is nothing that could hinder Him from doing that which He desires.

Second, this angel needed help from Michael one of the chief angels. God does not need help from anyone to carry out His plans, certainly not another angel.

Third, from the description given in this verse, Michael, who helped this particular angel, is a being of higher authority, or status, than the messenger who was hindered. This alone would rule out it being the Son of God.

Finally, the heavenly messenger was sent from heaven to bring the message. Angels are created beings who are sent from God, God Himself is the sender, not the messenger.

Previously, the angel Gabriel had been sent by God to reveal divine truth to the prophet Daniel.

> Then I heard a human voice coming from between the banks of the Ulai. It called out, "Gabriel, enable this person to understand the vision" (Daniel 8:16 NET).

Consequently, it was likely Gabriel was the heavenly personage who visited Daniel on this occasion.

This sums up the arguments each side presents in an attempt to understand exactly who it was that appeared to Daniel.

When all the facts are in, it seems that the heavenly being who visited Daniel was more likely an angel who resembled the glorified Christ but was merely His representative.

SUMMARY TO APPENDIX 2
DID THE SON OF GOD APPEAR TO DANIEL AS AN ANGEL? (DANIEL 10:1-6)

In the Book of Daniel, at a crucial time in the history of Israel, we have an episode where a man appeared to the prophet with a special message. From the appearance of the man, it is obvious that he was a heavenly being. Just exactly who he is has been a cause of much discussion.

There are two basic options, either this was a visit of the pre-incarnate Christ to Daniel, or it was the visitation of a mighty angel, possibly Gabriel.

The arguments for this being an appearance of the Son of God can be summed up as follows.

First, the description of the personage is similar to that which we read in Ezekiel. In that particular episode, it is clear that the prophet saw the glory of the Lord in heaven. The man he described was the Lord Himself.

This is similar to the description of the throne of God which we read in the Book of Revelation.

Add to this, the appearance of this angel to Daniel, is similar to the experience of Saul of Tarsus on the Damascus road.

Finally, the description of the personage fits with the way the glorified Christ is described in the first chapter of the Book of Revelation.

However, there are four major problems with this view. First, we are told that this particular angel was thwarted for three weeks by a demon before he could reach Daniel. This could never have happened if this heavenly messenger was an appearance of God Himself.

Also Michael the archangel had to help this personage in his struggle. This not only places this angel as a less powerful being than Michael, it show that whoever it is, he could not win the spiritual battle on his own. This alone would rule out it be God Himself who visited Daniel.

Finally, this messenger was sent by the Lord. In this context, it is another indication of a being that is inferior to God Himself.

All in all, it seems that the being described in this passage was an angel, probably Gabriel.

Are The Twenty Four Elders In The Book Of Revelation Humans Or Heavenly Beings?

In the Book of Revelation there is a unique description of personages in heaven known as the "twenty-four elders." They are described in this manner.

> In a circle around the throne were twenty-four other thrones, and seated on those thrones were twenty-four elders. They were dressed in white clothing and had golden crowns on their heads (Revelation 4:4 NET).

These elders appear a number of times in the Book of Revelation but are found nowhere else in the Bible. Their identity is much debated.

HEAVENLY BEINGS OR ANGELS?

Usually the question is framed in this manner: Are the twenty four elders humans or angels? However, this is an incorrect way of stating the question.

As we have observed, there are other heavenly beings that the Lord has created apart from the angels. This includes the living creatures, the cherubim and the seraphim. These particular beings seem to continually reside in heaven, while the angels are ministering sprits who are sent to various places to do the work of the Lord.

Since these twenty-four elders seem to remain in heaven while sitting upon thrones, "heavenly beings" would be a better way of describing these personages if they are not humans.

OPTION 1: HEAVENLY BEINGS

Many modern commentators believe that the twenty four elders are an order of heavenly being. There are a number of reasons as to why this is so.

WHITE APPAREL IS THE USUAL DRESS OF ANGELS

To begin with, they are wearing white apparel, this is the characteristic dress of angels. We will cite a few examples.

> Suddenly there was a violent earthquake, because an angel of the Lord descended from heaven and approached the tomb. He rolled back the stone and was sitting on it. His appearance was like lightning, and his robe was as white as snow (Matthew 28:2,3 HCSB).

The angel of the Lord was dressed in white.

> When they entered the tomb, they saw a young man dressed in a long white robe sitting on the right side; they were amazed and alarmed (Mark 16:5 HCSB).

One of the angels, who looked like a young man, had a long white robe.

> She saw two angels in white sitting there, one at the head and one at the feet, where Jesus' body had been lying (John 20:12 HCSB).

Again we have the emphasis of angels wearing white.

> While He was going, they were gazing into heaven, and suddenly two men in white clothes stood by them. They said,

"Men of Galilee, why do you stand looking up into heaven? This Jesus, who has been taken from you into heaven, will come in the same way that you have seen Him going into heaven" (Acts 1:10-12 HCSB).

The angels at Jesus' ascension, who are described as men, were also wearing white.

The dress of these elders is consistent with angelic dress in Scripture. While it is not specifically stated that the other heavenly beings in heaven are clothed in white, it seems to be a logical inference.

However, one could say in response that the other heavenly beings, seraphim, cherubim, and the four living creatures, are never specifically said to be wearing white garments. Therefore, it seems that this specific argument may not carry much weight.

THE SEPTUAGINT TRANSLATION OF ISAIAH 24:23

It is argued that the Septuagint, the Greek translation of the Hebrew Old Testament of Isaiah 24:23, has heavenly beings referred to as elders.

> Then the brick will be dissolved, and the wall will fall, because the Lord will reign in Zion and in Jerusalem, and before the elders he will be glorified (Isaiah 24:23 LXX).

However, the elders in this context could refer to humans, vice regents who will be there with the Lord at the time He sets up His kingdom. When this takes place, they will behold His glory. These human elders will have a similar role as the elders of Israel who beheld glory of the Lord on Mount Sinai. Consequently this is not a clear biblical reference of the word "elders" referring to some type of heavenly being.

JOHN CALLED THE ANGEL MY LORD

John called one of the elders "my lord."

> So I said to him, "My lord, you know the answer." Then he said to me, "These are the ones who have come out of the

great tribulation. They have washed their robes and made them white in the blood of the Lamb (Revelation 7:14 NET).

The fact that John addressed one of the elders in this manner has caused some to argue that they must be heavenly beings, not humans.

In answer to this, the term translated "lord" in the New Testament does not always have the connotation of some type of supernatural being. Humans are also addressed by this Greek term. Therefore, the fact that John addressed one of the elders in this manner does not necessarily make them something other than human.

THE ELDERS ARE GROUPED WITH THE FOUR LIVING BEINGS (CREATURES)

These elders are grouped with the angels, as well as the four living creatures, which everyone agrees are heavenly beings, not humans.

> And all the angels stood there in a circle around the throne and around the elders and the four living creatures, and they threw themselves down with their faces to the ground before the throne and worshiped God (Revelation 7:11 NET).

The elders are mentioned together with these four living beings, and the angels. In other words, while they are distinct from the angels, and the four living creatures, they are group with other heavenly beings which the Lord has created. This is one of the better arguments for them being non-human.

We also find them linked together with the four living creatures at the Second Coming of Christ.

> After these things I heard what sounded like the loud voice of a vast throng in heaven, saying, "Hallelujah! Salvation and glory and power belong to our God, because his judgments are true and just. For he has judged the great prostitute who corrupted the earth with her sexual immorality, and has

avenged the blood of his servants poured out by her own hands!" Then a second time the crowd shouted, "Hallelujah!" The smoke rises from her forever and ever. The twenty-four elders and the four living creatures threw themselves to the ground and worshiped God, who was seated on the throne, saying: "Amen! Hallelujah" (Revelation 19:1-4 NET).

In this instance, the elders are linked to the living creatures but there is no mention of angels in heaven with them.

THE APPARENT DISTINCTION BETWEEN THE ELDERS AND THE BRIDE OF CHRIST

There is something else we discover. When the Lord Jesus returns from heaven, His bride, the New Testament believers, the church will return with Him. They are called the "armies that were in heaven."

> Then I saw heaven opened, and there was a white horse. Its rider is called Faithful and True, and He judges and makes war in righteousness . . . . The armies that were in heaven followed Him on white horses, wearing pure white linen (Revelation 19:11,14 HCSB).

However, in Revelation 19 there seems to be a distinction between these believers returning with Christ and the twenty-four elders. At this time, the twenty-four elders are linked with the living creatures, and they remain in heaven.

In other words, they are not part of the armies of heaven, those returning with the Lord to the earth. This would seem to indicate that the twenty-four elders are not part of the group that makes up the New Testament Christians, since the entire group returns with the Lord to the earth.

Of course, one could say in response that the twenty-four elders are not New Testament believers but are made up of saints from the Old

ANGELS

Testament era. This would explain why they do not return with the New Testament Christians.

These are some of the reasons which have caused many to think that the elders are most likely heavenly beings, not humans.

OPTION 2: THE TWENTY FOUR ELDERS ARE A REDEEMED COMPANY OF HUMANS

While arguments are made for these elders to be a specific group of heavenly beings, the following arguments favor identifying the elders as humans, not as angels.

THIS IS THE OLDEST INTERPRETATION

First, this is the oldest interpretation of the identity of the elders. It goes back to a man named Victorinus of Pettau who died in A.D. 304. Therefore, some argue that this is the traditional interpretation.

IN THE BIBLE, THE TERM ELDERS IS USED OF HUMANS IN AUTHORITY

The term "Elders" is consistently used in both testaments to refer to humans. Indeed, in the Old Testament, it refers to men were had authority over certain cities. They would function as representatives for their communities. For example, we read the following in the Book of Deuteronomy.

> And all the elders of that city nearest to the slain man shall wash their hands over the heifer whose neck was broken in the valley (Deuteronomy 21:6 ESV).

In the New Testament, the Greek word can mean an older person as well as indicating one who has authority and prestige. Indeed, the leaders of the early church were called elders. We find the following words of the Apostle Paul to Titus.

> This is why I left you in Crete, so that you might put what remained into order, and appoint elders in every town as I directed you (Titus 1:5 ESV).

Therefore, in both testaments, the word "elder" has the specific meaning of humans who are in the place of ruling and authority. As we mentioned, this term is never used to designate angels or any other type of heavenly being anywhere in Scripture. The only exception may be Isaiah 24:23 which, as we observed, could very well be speaking of humans.

HEAVENLY BEINGS NEVER SIT UPON THRONES AND JUDGE

In Scripture, angels are never said to occupy thrones, as those who are in authority, to judge and rule the people. Instead, they minister to God's people in the role as messengers, not rulers.

On the other hand, the New Testament believers are promised to sit upon thrones as well as having some type of governmental authority or rulership in the world to come. We find the following promise which Jesus made to His disciples.

> Jesus said to them, "I assure you: In the Messianic Age, when the Son of Man sits on His glorious throne, you who have followed Me will also sit on 12 thrones, judging the 12 tribes of Israel" (Matthew 19:28 HCSB).

This promise is fulfilled in the Book of Revelation.

> Then I saw thrones, and people seated on them who were given authority to judge. I also saw the people who had been beheaded because of their testimony about Jesus and because of God's word, who had not worshiped the beast or his image, and who had not accepted the mark on their foreheads or their hands. They came to life and reigned with the Messiah for 1,000 years (Revelation 20:4 HCSB).

This is a point in favor of the elders being humans. However, if these heavenly beings are a distinct group of heavenly creatures apart from the angels, and with a higher ranking, then it is possible that they could be involved in carrying out God's judgment and rulership in some unspoken way. We simply are not told one way or the other.

CROWNS ARE NEVER LINKED TO ANGELS

In the Bible, crowns are never assigned to angels. In fact, they are specific rewards for believers in Christ. Paul wrote.

> Now everyone who competes exercises self- control in everything. However, they do it to receive a crown that will fade away, but we a crown that will never fade away (1 Corinthians 9:25 HCSB).

He wrote to the Thessalonians

> For who is our hope or joy or crown of boasting in the presence of our Lord Jesus at His coming? Is it not you? For you are our glory and joy (1 Thessalonians 2:19 HCSB).

James wrote something similar.

> A man who endures trials is blessed, because when he passes the test he will receive the crown of life that God has promised to those who love Him (James 1:12 HCSB).

Peter concurred.

> And when the chief Shepherd appears, you will receive the unfading crown of glory (1 Peter 5:4 HCSB).

Again, we could say in response that since the first option says that the twenty-four elders are a distinct order of heavenly being, and not angels, it does not matter that crowns are never linked to angels, a lesser ranked group of God's supernaturally created beings. In fact, the crowns may suggest a judicial function.

In response to this, we can note the following. While these higher ranked beings may indeed wear some type of crown, we are never told this in Scripture. Furthermore, the Greek word for crowns in Revelation 4:4 is *stephanos*, a victor's crown, that is, a trophy won at the games. This differs from the royal crown of governmental authority, the Greek word *diadema*. Therefore, the particular crowns these elders are wearing are not the type that were used in a judicial function.

CROWNS, THRONES AND WHITE CLOTHES ARE ALL PROMISED TO BELIEVERS

One of the seemingly decisive factors in determining the identity of the elders could be the three things which characterize them, crowns, thrones and white clothes. What we find from Scripture is that believers in Christ are promised these three things.

CROWNS

> Do not fear what you are about to suffer. Behold, the devil is about to throw some of you into prison, that you may be tested, and for ten days you will have tribulation. Be faithful unto death, and I will give you the crown of life … I am coming soon. Hold fast what you have, so that no one may seize your crown (Revelation 2:10; 3:11 ESV).

THRONES

> The one who conquers, I will grant him to sit with me on my throne, as I also conquered and sat down with my Father on his throne (Revelation 3:21 ESV).

WHITE CLOTHES

> The one who conquers will be clothed thus in white garments … I counsel you to buy from me gold refined by fire, so that you may be rich, and white garments so that you may clothe yourself and the shame of your nakedness may not be seen, and salve to anoint your eyes, so that you may see (Revelation 3:5,18 ESV).

This is a much better argument in support of the view that the twenty-four elders are humans. While angels are not promised any of these things, and other heavenly beings are never specifically said to sit upon thrones, wear crowns, or wear white for that matter, humans are promised all three of these things. This is seemingly the best argument for the elders to be some type of humans.

CONCLUSION

There is no easy answer to this question. Seemingly, the twenty-four elders may represent the New Testament believers who have been rewarded for their faithfulness and endurance. The Lord has promised to give them the "victor's crown."

> Do not be afraid of what you are about to suffer. I tell you, the devil will put some of you in prison to test you, and you will suffer persecution for ten days. Be faithful, even to the point of death, and I will give you life as your victor's crown . . . In the same way, the victor will be dressed in white clothes, and I will never erase his name from the book of life but will acknowledge his name before My Father and before His angels (Revelation 2:10, 3:5 HCSB).

On the other hand, since these twenty-four elders are always linked with heavenly beings, we could assume that they are a different order of God's creation apart from the angels, the living creatures, the seraphim, and the cherubim.

Given each of these possibilities, there does not seem to be enough evidence one way or another, to make a definite conclusion. They are not angels, but they could be a different order of heavenly beings.

SUMMARY TO APPENDIX 3
ARE THE TWENTY FOUR ELDERS IN THE BOOK OF REVELATION HUMANS OR HEAVENLY BEINGS?

In the Book of Revelation, there is a unique designation of twenty-four beings sitting on thrones in heaven. They are known as "elders." This is the only place in Scripture where this particular description is given to us. Their identity is one that is disputed. Indeed, some people think they are heavenly beings, while others believe they are humans.

The case for them being heavenly beings can be simply listed as follows. First, they are wearing white, the color of another type of heavenly being, angels.

Second, they are always linked in heaven with other heavenly beings, never humans.

Third, when Jesus Christ returns, these twenty-four elders seem to remain in heaven while all the believers in Christ return with Him to the earth. This would seem to indicate a distinction between them and New Testament believers.

These arguments, among others, have convinced many that the elders are heavenly beings, not humans.

On the other hand, these twenty-four "elders" sit on thrones, and rule while wearing white garments. These three things are specifically promised to the New Testament believers. This may indicate that it is New Testament Christians whom these twenty-four elders represent.

Add to this, the Bible, in both testaments, uses the word "elder" to refer to humans who are in place of rulership. We never find the word used of angels or other heavenly beings.

In sum, it is difficult to decide exactly whom they represent. Either view is possible.

APPENDIX 4

Does Revelation 5:9-10, In Some Translations, Solve The Problem As To The Identity Of The Twenty-Four Elders?

The identity of the twenty-four elders could be solved if a particular translation of Revelation 5:9-10 is accepted as valid. For example, we read the following.

> Now when He had taken the scroll, the four living creatures and the twenty-four elders fell down before the Lamb, each having a harp, and golden bowls full of incense, which are the prayers of the saints. And they sang a new song, saying: "You are worthy to take the scroll, And to open its seals; For You were slain, And have redeemed us to God by Your blood Out of every tribe and tongue and people and nation, And have made us kings and priests to our God; And we shall reign on the earth (Revelation 5:8-10 NKJV).

In Revelation 5:9 these elders in heaven worship the Lamb because, they say, "You were slain and You have redeemed us for God By Your blood." In Revelation 5:10 they say, "And you have made us kings and priests; And we shall reign on the earth."

The King James Version reads similar in this verse.

> Thou art worthy to take the book, and to open the seals thereof: for thou wast slain, and hast redeemed us to God by

> thy blood out of every kindred, and tongue, and people, and nation. And hast made us unto our God kings and priests: and we shall reign on the earth (Revelation 5:9,10 KJV).

This translation asserts that the twenty-four elders in heaven are those whom Jesus Christ redeemed, or bought, by His death on the cross. Indeed, twice they sing that the Lord redeemed "us" and they also sing that "we" shall reign on the earth.

Since the Lord only redeemed humans, and not angels or any other heavenly being by His death, these verses make it clear that the elders are humans, not some other type of heavenly creation of God.

OTHER TRANSLATIONS ARE DIFFERENT

However, almost every other English translation of this verse reads differently. For example, consider the following way in which other versions translate these two verses.

> They were singing a new song: "You are worthy to take the scroll and to open its seals because you were killed, and at the cost of your own blood you have purchased for God persons from every tribe, language, people, and nation. You have appointed them as a kingdom and priests to serve our God, and they will reign on the earth" (Revelation 5:9-10 NET).

And they sang a new song, saying: "You are worthy to take the scroll

> and to open its seals, because you were slain, and with your blood you purchased for God persons from every tribe and language and people and nation. You have made them to be a kingdom and priests to serve our God, and they will reign on the earth" (Revelation 5:9-10 NIV).

Other translations such as the ESV, HCSB, NLT, and CEV read something similar.

According to these translations, the twenty-four elders are not part of the redeemed but are a distinct group of heavenly beings. Indeed, the song they sing proclaims that the Lord redeemed "persons" from every tribe" . . . . "You have made them to be a kingdom and priests" and they will reign on the earth.

In sum, instead of "us," "us," and "we" that is found in the KJV and NKJV the other translations read "persons" "them" and "they."

WHY DO THEY TRANSLATE THIS VERSE DIFFERENTLY?

The NKJV and KJV translation assumes the genuineness of the Greek pronoun haymas, translated as "us" in Revelation 5:9 and 5:10. The other English translations believe this word does not belong in the text in either instance. In the Revelation 5:9 there is no direct object in the verse. In other words it has to be supplied. Consequently, this would leave the verse without a direct object, without some word explaining whom the Lord bought with His blood. They supply the word "persons." The translation note from the NET Bible explains why.

The word "persons" is not in the Greek text, but is implied. Direct objects were often omitted in Greek when clear from the context (Translation Note On Revelation 5:9 from NET Bible).

Why do they do this? The main argument for excluding the word translated as "us" in verse 9 is found in verse 10. It reads.

You have made "them" to be a kingdom and priests to our God. . . . and "they" will reign

Most manuscripts read "them" in this verse while only a few have the word "us." They also accept the reading which says "they" will reign on the earth rather that "we" will reign. Again, most manuscripts have the word "they" and not "we."

To sum up, the variations in the Greek text. In verse 9 some manuscripts have the Greek word for us while other manuscripts do not have a direct object. However, since most manuscripts of verse 10 have the words "them" and "they" in the text, the translators supply the word "persons" in verse 9 to make it clear whom the Lord bought.

Therefore, in this translation, the elders, singing the song of the redeemed, do not include themselves with these believers. In fact, they make the distinction between themselves and those whom Christ bought with His blood. If this is what these verses are teaching, then the twenty-four elders would not be part of the New Testament believers for whom Christ died.

WHICH ARE THE CORRECT READINGS?

While most English translations read "persons" rather than "us" in Revelation 5:9, the evidence for "us" being the genuine reading is impressive. In fact, the great majority of Greek manuscripts, early translations, and the writings of the early Christians, known as the church fathers, include the word. In fact, the earliest manuscript of Revelation which contains this verse, Codex Sinaiticus, does include this reading "us."

The evidence against the inclusion of "us" is largely internal. The problem is that does agree with "them" and "they" in verse ten. In other words, those singing would not say in verse nine, "you have redeemed us" and then in verse ten say "you have redeemed them." Since the pronouns conflict with one another, the pronoun "us" is omitted in verse nine to make the translation consistent.

Furthermore, the evidence for the NKJV and KJV readings in verse 10, "us" and "we" have little manuscript support. It seems clear that in verse ten "them and "they" are the proper reading of the text.

A POSSIBLE SOLUTION

However, there is a possible solution which keeps both the pronoun "us" in verse nine, as in the NKJV and the KJV, and the pronouns "them" and "they" in verse ten, as in modern translations, which makes sense in the context. This solution was offered a 19th century commentator on the Book of Revelation, Moses Stuart.

He argued that verses 9 and 10 contain what is known as a responsive or antiphonal praise. Stuart observed that in verses 9 and 10, there are two distinct groups who are worshiping God. They are the "four living creatures and the "twenty-four elders."

His solution was as follows. In Revelation 5:9, the twenty-four elders, a redeemed company of believers, are praising the Lamb for redeeming "us to God." In other words, they are praising the Lord for their salvation through Christ.

However, in Revelation 5:10, there is a different group singing; it is the four living creatures. These heavenly beings then respond to the twenty-four elders by saying with, "You have made them to be a kingdom and priests." In other words, what is recorded in Revelation 5:9 is the song of the 24 elders. However, in verse Revelation 5:10 the singers are the four living creatures.

This understanding of the passage would have the four living creatures acknowledging that the twenty-four elders were part of the redeemed company of believers.

The result would be that the text in verse nine would read like as the KJV and NKJV translations. However, in verse ten, it would read like the modern translations.

While this is not the only way in which these verses could be understood, it does solve the problem of the conflicting pronouns. Furthermore, it would make the twenty-four elders human beings, part of the New Testament church.

As we mentioned, this is a "possible" way of understanding these verses but it is not the only way. Consequently, nobody should build their case for the twenty-four elders being redeemed humans solely upon this particular understanding of these two verses.

SUMMARY TO APPENDIX 4
DOES REVELATION 5:9-10, IN SOME TRANSLATIONS, SOLVE THE PROBLEM AS TO THE IDENTITY OF THE TWENTY-FOUR ELDERS?

The identity of the twenty-four elders in the Book of Revelation could be solved if the King James and New King James translation of Revelation 5:9 is accepted as original. It has the twenty-four elders including themselves in the company of the redeemed, those for whom Jesus Christ died. The translation has them singing that Christ redeemed "us."

Since the Lord only died to redeem sinful humans, and not angels or other heavenly beings, this would make the twenty-four elders human beings.

While the word translated "us" in Revelation 5:9 is in the great majority of Greek manuscripts, as well as in early translations of this verse, and the writings of the early Christians, it is rejected by modern translations. The reason for this is because the pronoun "us" does not line up with the pronouns "them" and "they" in verse ten. Modern translations understand the twenty-four elders as praising the Lord for redeeming "humans;" they are not including themselves for whom Christ died.

However, there is a proposed solution to this issue. It was first offered long ago by Moses Stuart in the 19th century. It can be summed up as follows.

Two groups are praising the Lord in Revelation 5:9, the twenty-four elders as well as the four living creatures. Nobody denies this. Therefore, if we assume that the twenty-four elders are singing praises to the Lord for their redemption in verse nine, it is possible that the second group, the four living creatures, are acknowledging this reality in verse ten.

In other words, it is only the four living creatures who are singing the song in verse ten. In doing this, they are also thanking the Lord for redeeming "them," the twenty-four elders.

This solution accepts the Greek text as read in the Greek majority of the manuscripts which includes the reading "us" in verse nine and the words "them" and "they" in verse ten. Consequently, the KJV an NKJV has it correct in verse nine while the modern translations have it right in verse ten.

While not the only possible solution, it does seem to be a simple way to solve the problem of the conflicting pronouns without resorting to removing the pronoun "us" in verse nine; which is found in practically every manuscript of the Book of Revelation.

However, since this is a difficult question, with a number of proposed solutions, one should not build their case concerning the identity of the twenty-four elders solely on this verse.

About The Author

Don Stewart is a graduate of Biola University and Talbot Theological Seminary (with the highest honors).

Don is a best-selling and award-winning author having authored, or co-authored, over seventy books. This includes the best-selling *Answers to Tough Questions*, with Josh McDowell, as well as the award-winning book *Family Handbook of Christian Knowledge: The Bible*. His various writings have been translated into over thirty different languages and have sold over a million copies.

Don has traveled around the world proclaiming and defending the historic Christian faith. He has also taught both Hebrew and Greek at the undergraduate level and Greek at the graduate level.

OUR NEXT BOOK IN THE UNSEEN WORLD SERIES:
VOLUME 2

Evil Angels, Demons, And The Occult

In the next book in our series on the unseen world we examine the topics of evil angels, demons and the occult. We will look at questions such as the following.

Who Are The Evil Angels?

When Did The Angelic Rebellion Occur?

What Are Demons?

Where Did Demons Originate?

Were The Sons Of God Fallen Angels Who Married Earthly Women? (Genesis 6)